THE
minimalist
entertains

THE

minimalist
entertains

FORTY SEASONAL MENUS FOR DINNER PARTIES, COCKTAIL PARTIES, BARBECUES, AND MORE

MARK BITTMAN

Broadway Books
New York

Broadway Books titles may be purchased for business or promotional use or for special sales. For information, please write to: Special Markets Department, Random House, Inc., 1745 Broadway, New York, NY 10019.

PRINTED IN THE UNITED STATES OF AMERICA

BROADWAY BOOKS and its logo, a letter B bisected on the diagonal, are trademarks of Broadway Books, a division of Random House, Inc.

Visit our website at www.broadwaybooks.com

Book design by Elizabeth Rendfleisch

Library of Congress Cataloging-in-Publication Data

Bittman, Mark.
The minimalist entertains / Mark Bittman.
p. cm.
(alk. paper)
1. Entertaining. 2. Dinners and dining. 3. Quick and easy cookery. 4. Menus.
I. Title.

TX731 .B48 2003

642'.4—dc21   2002026288

ISBN 0-7679-1193-8

1 3 5 7 9 10 8 6 4 2

"The Minimalist" columns originally appeared in the *New York Times*. Reprinted by permission. Inquiries concerning permission to reprint any column or portion thereof should be directed to The New York Times Company, News Services Division, The Times Agency, Ninth Floor, 229 West 43rd Street, New York, New York 10036.

"The Minimalist" is a trademark of The New York Times Company and is used under license.

To minimalist cooks everywhere,
with gratitude

Contents

⚗

autumn

winter

Acknowledgments

For the entire run of "The Minimalist," my *New York Times* column—now six years—I've been lucky to have great editors, starting with Trish Hall and Rick Flaste and continuing in the person of Michaelene Busico. These days, happily, my editors are Sam Sifton, Barbara Graustark, and (sometimes) my friend Eric Asimov. All have been encouraging and supportive, and together we've watched "The Mini" grow and thrive.

The Minimalist Entertains was launched a couple of years ago— it was Barbara's idea—as an expanded, monthly version of the weekly column, centered (obviously) on entertaining. It was at that point that I began an ostensibly formal entertaining schedule, inviting friends over more-or-less weekly as I tested not only the recipes in this book but the way they work together. These friends seemed to have a good enough time, so I won't thank all of them individually (they know who they are), but I do owe them a broad thanks, because although I'm quite sure the menus presented here will work for you, at the beginning many of them did not work that well for me, and it was my friends who suffered through some of those evenings while I was ironing out the kinks.

However, some special friends and colleagues have been there for me and helped me out in recent years, and I want to thank them especially: Karen Baar, Mitchell Orfuss, Naomi Glauberman, John

Bancroft, Madeline Meacham, David Paskin, Pamela Hort, Jack Hitt, Semeon Tsalbins, Susan Moldow, Bill Shinker, Mary Elizabeth Webb (and all the crew at the *Today* show), Nancy Newhouse, Jim Nelson, Adam Rapoport, Joe and Kim McGrath, Fred Zolna, Sherry Slade, Katherine Lanpher, Lisa Sanders, Genevieve Ko, Glory Gallo, Russ Parsons, Faith Middleton, Evan Kleinman and the folks at KCRW, and John Owen and his staff at Travel-Holiday.

I have been blessed, too, with great colleagues at Broadway Books: my editor Jennifer Josephy, my publisher Steve Rubin, the great publicity department—especially Suzanne Herz and Jenny Danquist—and Jackie Everly-Warren, Catherine Pollock, book designer Elizabeth Rendfleisch, Rebecca Holland, and Laura Marshall. My agent, Angela Miller, is simply the best, and has been a terrific influence in my life for over a decade; huge thanks to her.

As always, special thanks to my most frequent companions, John H. Willoughby, John Ringwald, and Alisa X. Smith, all of whom give me invaluable love and perspective on a daily basis, and newfound confidence in the occasionally intimidating world of entertaining.

As for Kate and Emma, you are the best.

Introduction

"Entertaining" can be an awesome responsibility or a pleasure. Until recently, I believed that only people like Fred Astaire and Martha Stewart entertained. It was my lot, on the other hand, when occasionally seized by obligation, altruism, guilt, or all three, to gather my wits, strength, and slightly-above-average cooking skills and stumble through putting together a dinner party. On those occasions, I worried about everything, from my flimsy stainless steel to my unmatched chairs. When it got to the food, I was even worse; I could become downright hysterical when I couldn't find that special fish for a bouillabaisse or live shrimp for a stir-fry.

The result was that—and this, I have since found out, is a common ailment—I worked harder than anyone else (or felt like I did; I said ailment, remember). At least, I thought, I could try to make the food incredible.

Of course this meant never, ever scheduling a dinner party for a weeknight, including Friday (or Sunday, really, since I was usually a wreck afterward), because I needed at least a day or two to cook without the distractions of real life. It meant shopping on Thursday, prepping and cooking on Friday, and cooking and performing last-minute tasks—like driving twenty miles to find some "absolutely essential" ingredient—all day Saturday, until the fateful hour, by which time, like just about everyone else who cooks, I was nervous and exhausted.

Need I say that these were difficult, overly ambitious affairs? Though I eventually realized that the only way to make a dinner party glorious was to hire help, my only help came from my equally overmatched family members, and my guests themselves. When following the directions for a "real" dinner party, this never seemed enough.

There had to be a better way, I came to think, and my discovery of this happened, as things often do, by accident. The turning point was the scariest dinner party I ever held, one at which I finally realized that it was my own standards, and not those of my guests, that made me work like a fiend and worry neurotically. This revelation changed the way I entertain forever.

What happened on this occasion was that I completely forgot that, as a return of favor, I had agreed to throw a party for a friend and five of his friends—a total of eight people. When the day arrived, and the friend interrupted a midafternoon slumber with a phone call, asking what time he and his party should arrive, I first caught my breath, blurted out "six-thirty" (we eat early in the suburbs), and then quickly changed it to eight. I hung up and pessimistically looked in the refrigerator, where there was the lone chicken I had bought for dinner that night, along with some premixed mesclun. Obviously this wasn't going to cut it.

I headed to the supermarket, thinking furiously. There was no time for new recipes, no time for research, no time for anything but a simple weeknight dinner for four multiplied by two. In other words, the minimalist entertains—the birth of this book.

The details of my self-rescue are not that impressive: I had originally been planning to prepare chicken with vinegar, a classic French peasant dish, along with the salad greens and the pan-crisped potato cubes my family adored. I decided to build only slightly on this menu, adding some kind of starter, a bread, and a dessert—chocolate mousse seemed best—as a desperate attempt to provide not only some festivity but the suggestion that I had actually given the whole thing a great deal of consideration.

By the time I arrived at the supermarket, my job was pretty easy: I bought more chicken, more salad greens, and some cream. In what has become typical fashion, I bought three kinds of olives and a dry salami—my idea of a good appetizer—and a couple of loaves of bread.

Since I was pressed for time, I decided to try a "new" chocolate mousse recipe that a friend had taught me, one in which you simply folded together chocolate ganache and whipped cream; she swore by it, and it was certainly easier and faster than my more old-fashioned version using eggs. I made that first, so it could chill, and almost instantly could see that I'd be disappointed. Maybe I had done something wrong (isn't that always our first thought? yet sometimes recipes plain don't work), but the ganache made the mousse far stiffer than I liked. It looked something like volcanic rock, but it was too late to do anything about that. I added it to my list of worries and thanked myself for the foresight that led me to buy enough cream to whip some and cover the mousse's top; at least the initial appearance wasn't going to be an issue. (For my original recipe, see page 14.)

Then I marinated the olives (see page 66), a foolproof situation. I cut up the salami, another one. I ate some. Then I cooked.

Of course it wasn't too bad, and, really, why should it have been? It may not have shouted "I killed myself for you people," but when eight o'clock arrived, as it inevitably does, so did my guests, who drank wine while nibbling salami and devouring the olives. The olives, it turned out, were symbolic of the entire event, enjoyed because they tasted good and were, though simple, unusual.

I realize this is anticlimactic, but everything was well received. In fact, the dinner was a smashing success, with my guests raving about the same food that on any given night of the year my children might have complained about. Although it was all imperfect (my judgment; my guests seemed to think everything was splendid, including the ultraordinary salad), and far from a restaurant-quality meal, who says that we have to deliver either near-perfection or food that costs a hundred dollars a person? That is not—really—what home entertaining is about.

All of this was a lesson I never forgot, one that changed my life, not for the near-disaster that I feared but for the one that did not happen. In the intervening years, I have yet to develop a foolproof method of getting all dates into my calendar, but I have learned that dinner parties need not take days of work. Now I limit my hysteria to only the last couple of hours before the guests arrive; I also limit most of the work to that time period, as you'll see here. It may not be Martha, but it usually requires only a little bit of volunteer help, it looks pretty good, and the food tastes great.

At the risk of being formulaic, let me say that there are a few basic rules that I've found are worth following when combining entertaining with a will to remain healthy and happy. First, keep your expectations reasonable while exercising good judgment. For judgment, I might say "restraint." My problem with entertaining, and that of most people I know, was an excess of ambition. (We come by this honestly, as there is a tradition of this in the United States. It's called "Thanksgiving.") Without significant help, and I don't just mean someone to wash the dishes, it is a challenge to prepare a meal that includes more than two complicated dishes. Indeed, on anything except a special occasion, when you might set aside four hours or more to be in the kitchen, it's nearly impossible to prepare a meal that includes more than a single fairly complex dish.

The Minimalist Entertains is based on these principles. Some of the menus contain store-bought items (marked with a ﾧ) like bread and ice cream. Few offer more than one complicated dish (and, as those of you who are familiar with my work know, my definition of complicated is pretty simple), and many offer the option of dropping a dish or even two while still maintaining a degree of splendor—well, if not splendor, then at least festivity. (In many of the Keys to Success sections, I offer suggestions for adding a dish or two, should you want to make a given menu more elaborate.)

I also provide wine suggestions, but with these caveats: Wine can not only ease the flow of conversation, it makes food taste better. (Let's not forget, however, that part of the reason for this is that it impairs judgment.) It is not an essential part of a good meal but a fine optional addition, and one that many of us have come to consider routine. Which is all well and good; but unless you're comfortable with the jargon of wine, or want to learn about it, don't get too obsessive about it or let it make you too uptight. My suggestions are as general as possible, because I strongly believe that except for fanatics, who don't need my suggestions anyway (they know far more about the subject than I do), wine choices should be simple and straightforward.

The Minimalist Entertains differs in a few ways from its predecessors, *The Minimalist Cooks at Home* and *The Minimalist Cooks Dinner*. Most obviously, this book is organized by menus and seasons. There are forty menus, ten for each season, containing recipes for starters, entrées, main courses, and desserts. Although the summer menus feature a great deal of grilling, and the winter ones braising, do not take the seasonal restrictions too seriously; there is a lot of overlap, and many recipes are suited to any time of year.

Most recipes are designed to serve eight. In the vast majority, cutting all the ingredients in half will produce a fine recipe for four; in the remaining 10 percent or so, you may have to make some minor adjustments, but they will likely be obvious. In any case, I felt that it was safer to offer recipes that gave the quantity you were most likely to be using, instead of those serving four with instructions for doubling. Note that the serving size is usually designed to suit the menu; in other words, recipes for starters produce a smaller portion than recipes for main courses. When there are two main courses, each is scaled back in size a bit. In every case there is plenty of food. (When amounts appear large, remember you are cooking for a crowd; a half-stick of butter divided among eight people is not a lot of butter.)

Entertaining, as I said, can be a responsibility or a pleasure; usually, it's a little of each. I hope *The Minimalist Entertains* helps you shoulder the former and maximize the latter. It took me a long time to remember that good food, prepared with a modicum of care and thought, is appreciated by anyone who likes to eat. My grandmother knew this, but in the thirty years since I cooked with her I seemed to have forgotten it. It's a rediscovery I'm happy to have made.

Mark Bittman
Woodbridge, Connecticut
Spring 2003

spring

celebrating spring's arrival

RAW BEET SALAD

SAUTÉED RED SNAPPER WITH RHUBARB SAUCE

NEW POTATOES WITH BUTTER AND MINT

COEURS À LA CRÈME WITH STRAWBERRIES

Here is a menu that could not be made in any season
other than spring—at least not with truly fresh ingredients. Mint
is up out of the ground, strawberries are everywhere, rhubarb
is at the height of its short run, and beets are young, small, and
delicious. The meal is a simple festival.

KEYS TO SUCCESS

- To prepare the rhubarb, first "string" it. Hold the stalk in one hand. In the other, cut through the end with a small knife, stopping it short of cutting all the way through by pressing the flat of the blade against your thumb. Pull down the length of the stalk and the strings will come with it. This is a refinement, but a worthwhile one.

- For the snapper, substitute sea or striped bass, grouper, or rockfish.

- To make this menu somewhat more elaborate, add a soup, like Pan-Roasted Asparagus Soup with Tarragon (page 18) or Pea-and-Ginger Soup (page 30).

WINE

A crisp white would be best, like a Chablis or comparable California Chardonnay, or even something lighter, like Pinot Grigio.

THE TIMETABLE

- The dessert should be made the day before, so that will be out of the way except for the final assembly, which you can tackle while your guests relax for a little while after dinner.

- Prepare the beets first and let them sit while you start the potatoes and the rhubarb sauce.

- When the potatoes are nearly done, toss the beets with their dressing. Finish the potatoes and cook the fish at the same time; serve beets, potatoes, and fish together.

raw beet salad

Use young, small beets if you can find them. And wear an apron or old clothes; you will inevitably spatter some juice.

MAKES 8 SERVINGS

TIME: 20 MINUTES

2 pounds beets, preferably small

2 large shallots

Salt and freshly ground black pepper

1 tablespoon Dijon mustard, or to taste

2 tablespoons extra virgin olive oil

$1/4$ cup sherry vinegar or other good strong vinegar

Minced fresh parsley, dill, chervil, rosemary, or tarragon

1. Peel the beets and the shallots. Combine them in the bowl of a food processor fitted with the metal blade, and pulse carefully until the beets are chopped; do not puree. (Or grate the beets by hand and mince the shallots; combine.) Scrape into a bowl.

2. Toss with the salt, pepper, mustard, oil, and vinegar. Taste, and adjust the seasoning. Toss in the herbs, and serve.

sautéed red snapper with rhubarb sauce

The addition of saffron not only adds a mysterious flavor but gives the rhubarb a golden glow. Saffron is expensive, but not outrageous if bought in quantity; an ounce will last you years.

MAKES 8 SERVINGS

TIME: 40 MINUTES

2 pounds rhubarb, rinsed and trimmed, strings removed

2/3 cup sugar, or to taste

Large pinch of saffron, optional

Salt and freshly ground black pepper

1/4 cup olive oil

1/4 cup unsalted butter or use more oil

Eight 6-ounce fillets red snapper

Chopped fresh mint or parsley, optional

1. Combine the rhubarb, sugar, and saffron, if you are using it, in a medium saucepan, cover, and turn the heat to low. Cook, stirring only occasionally, for about 20 minutes, or until the rhubarb becomes saucy. Add salt and pepper to taste and a little more sugar if necessary; if the mixture is very soupy continue to cook a little longer to make it thicker.

2. When you judge the rhubarb to be nearly done, put a large skillet, preferably nonstick, over medium-high heat. (You can either use two skillets or cook in batches; undercook the first batch slightly and keep it warm in a 200°F oven while you cook the second batch.) A minute later, add the oil and butter (you may need a bit more of each if using two pans); when the butter foam subsides, add the fillets, skin side down. Cook for 4 to 5 minutes, or until the fish is nearly done; turn carefully and lightly brown the flesh side. Transfer to a plate lined with paper towels to absorb excess oil.

3. Serve the fish napped with a bit of the sauce and garnished, if you like, with the herb.

new potatoes
with butter and mint

Mint makes a huge difference here, countering the potatoes' earthiness with its bright flavor.

MAKES 8 SERVINGS

TIME: 40 MINUTES

About 4 pounds new red or white potatoes, the smaller the better, skins on and scrubbed

Several mint sprigs, plus minced fresh mint leaves

2 tablespoons unsalted butter, or more to taste

1. Place the potatoes in a pot with salted water to cover; turn the heat to high and bring to a boil. Add the mint sprigs and turn the heat down to medium. Cook at a gentle boil until the potatoes are nice and tender, 20 to 40 minutes depending on their size.

2. Drain the potatoes and return them to the pot over the lowest heat possible. Add the butter and cook, shaking the pan occasionally, until all traces of moisture have disappeared, about 5 minutes. Garnish with the minced mint leaves and serve hot.

coeurs à la crème with strawberries

"Hearts of Cream" (heart-shaped molds are traditional), a lovely, classic dessert, and one that takes very little attention or work.

MAKES 8 SERVINGS

TIME: 24 HOURS, LARGELY UNATTENDED

1 pound cream cheese

2 cups whole-milk yogurt

2 teaspoons vanilla extract

1 1/2 cups sugar, or more if needed

2 quarts strawberries, rinsed, hulled, and sliced

1. Use a fork or blender to cream together the cream cheese, yogurt, vanilla, and half the sugar. (If you use a blender and the mixture is too thick, add a little heavy cream or milk.) The mixture should be quite smooth. Place in a fine-mesh strainer lined with cheesecloth or a clean dish towel, and place the strainer over a bowl. Refrigerate until ready to serve.

2. About a half hour before serving, toss the strawberries with the remaining sugar and let sit at room temperature. Turn the cream cheese mixture out onto a plate and divide into eight portions or place some of the mixture in each of eight bowls. Mix the berries, if you like, with a little more sugar.

3. Serve the coeurs à la crème topped with the berry mixture.

an elegant sit-down dinner

SCALLOP SEVICHE

COQ AU VIN WITH PRUNES

ROASTED ASPARAGUS WITH PARMESAN

BREAD

CHOCOLATE MOUSSE

This is an impressive, white-tablecloth (though you can serve it with no tablecloth, of course), restaurant-quality kind of meal. Although it is not especially challenging, each dish is a small gem.

KEYS TO SUCCESS

■ If it's not too late in the season (it usually ends in March), try getting true bay ("Nantucket") scallops. If you cannot, don't fret; fresh sea scallops are also great.

■ If you'd like to make this menu somewhat more extensive with just a tiny bit more work, add Herbed Green Salad with Nut Vinaigrette (page 61).

WINE

Two would be best, a light, simple white, like Pinot Grigio, with the scallops, and the best red you can find for the chicken and asparagus course—a great Burgundy would not be out of place here.

THE TIMETABLE

■ Get the Chocolate Mousse out of the way as early as you can, so you don't have to bother with it while you're preparing the rest of the dishes. It can be made a day in advance.

■ Do all your chopping and dicing at once, then turn your attention to browning the chicken. Once that's done, you can assemble the asparagus and get it ready for the oven. While the chicken is simmering, put together the seviche.

■ Roast the asparagus while serving the seviche and allowing the chicken to finish cooking (once it's done, the chicken will hold for a while over low heat).

scallop seviche

This is a true seviche, one in which the scallops are "cooked" by the acidity of the citrus.

1 pound perfectly fresh sea scallops, cut into $1/4$-inch dice

3 tablespoons peeled and minced bell pepper, preferably a combination of red, yellow, and green

1 teaspoon minced lemon zest

1 tablespoon fresh orange juice

1 tablespoon fresh lemon juice

Salt

Cayenne to taste

2 tablespoons minced cilantro, optional

1. Toss together all the ingredients, except the cilantro, and let sit at room temperature for 15 minutes.

2. Taste, adjust the seasoning, and serve, garnished with the cilantro, if you like.

coq au vin with prunes

The chicken must be well browned before proceeding with the dish, and in this instance there is no hurrying the process: Take your time and brown each piece well; especially if you're cooking for 8 or more, this will take a while, as you'll have to brown in batches.

MAKES 8 SERVINGS

TIME: 60 MINUTES

2 tablespoons olive oil

2 chickens, cut into serving pieces

Salt and freshly ground black pepper

2 large onions, chopped

$^1/_2$ cup minced salt pork or bacon, optional

1 tablespoon minced garlic

$1^1/_2$ pounds pitted prunes

1 bottle Burgundy, Pinot Noir, or other fruity red wine

4 tablespoons ($^1/_2$ stick) unsalted butter, optional

Minced fresh parsley

1. Put the oil in a large skillet, preferably nonstick, and turn the heat to medium-high. A minute later, add as many of the chicken pieces as will fit without crowding, skin side down. Cook, rotating the pieces and adjusting the heat as necessary to cook them evenly, until nicely browned on the skin side, about 5 minutes; turn and brown on the other side(s). As the pieces are done, sprinkle them with salt and pepper, transfer them to a large casserole, and add the remaining pieces.

2. When all the chicken is browned, add the onions to the fat remaining in the skillet; cook over medium-high heat, stirring occasionally, until softened, 5 minutes or so, then transfer them to the casserole. Add the salt pork, if you're using it, and cook, stirring occasionally, until brown and crisp, about 5 minutes; transfer to the casserole and drain all but 1 tablespoon of the fat. Turn the heat to medium and add the garlic and, 30 seconds later, the prunes. Cook for a minute, stirring once or twice, then add to the casserole.

3. Turn the heat under the skillet to high and add half the wine. Cook, stirring and scraping the bottom of

(continued)

the pan to remove any solid particles there, until the wine is reduced by half. Pour into the casserole along with the remaining wine. Turn the heat under the casserole to high and bring to a boil; stir, then reduce the heat to low and cover. Simmer, stirring once or twice, until the chicken is done, about 30 minutes. Remove the top, stir in the optional butter, and raise the heat to high; cook until the sauce thickens a bit. Taste and adjust the seasoning if necessary; garnish with parsley and serve.

roasted asparagus
with parmesan

You want thin asparagus here, so you don't have to peel or parboil it.

MAKES 8 SERVINGS

TIME: 25 MINUTES

2 thick slices good bread, about 2 ounces

1 chunk Parmesan cheese, about 2 ounces

3 pounds thin asparagus, more or less

6 tablespoons unsalted butter, extra virgin olive oil, or a combination

Salt and freshly ground black pepper

1. Preheat the oven to 500°F; while it's preheating, put the bread in there, and check it frequently until it is lightly toasted and dry. Coarsely grind or grate the bread and Parmesan together (a small food processor is perfect for this)—if possible, keep the crumbs from becoming as small as commercial bread crumbs.

2. Rinse the asparagus and break off their woody bottoms. Lay them in a baking dish or roasting pan that will accommodate them in two or three layers. Toss with bits of the butter, sprinkle lightly with salt and pepper, and place in the oven.

3. Roast for 5 minutes, then shake the pan to redistribute the butter. Roast another 5 minutes, then test the asparagus for doneness by piercing a spear with the point of a sharp knife; it is done when the knife enters the asparagus but still meets a little resistance. You can prepare the recipe in advance up to this point as long as a couple of hours before serving; allow the asparagus to sit at room temperature during that time.

4. Turn on the broiler and place the rack as close as possible to the heating element. Sprinkle the bread crumb mixture over the asparagus. Carefully brown the topping—it will only take a minute or two—and serve the asparagus hot or at room temperature.

chocolate mousse

The richest, most elegant dessert you can make with so little work.

MAKES 8 SERVINGS

TIME: 30 MINUTES, PLUS TIME TO CHILL

3 tablespoons unsalted butter

6 ounces bittersweet or semisweet chocolate, chopped

5 eggs, separated

$^1/_2$ cup sugar

$^3/_4$ cup heavy cream

1 teaspoon vanilla extract

1. Use a double boiler or a small saucepan over low heat to melt the butter and chocolate together. Just before the chocolate finishes melting, remove it from the stove and beat with a wooden spoon until smooth.

2. Transfer the chocolate mixture to a bowl and beat in the egg yolks with a whisk. Place the bowl in the re-frigerator.

3. Beat the egg whites with half the sugar until they hold stiff peaks but are not dry. Set aside. Beat the cream with the remaining sugar and the vanilla until it holds soft peaks.

4. Stir a couple of spoonfuls of the whites into the chocolate mixture to lighten it a bit, then fold in the remaining whites thoroughly but gently. Fold in the cream and refrigerate until chilled. If you are in a hurry, divide the mousse among eight cups; it will chill much faster. Serve within a day of making.

a simple
spring dinner

PAN-ROASTED ASPARAGUS SOUP WITH TARRAGON

BROILED SALMON WITH BEURRE NOISETTE

PAN-CRISPED POTATOES

RICOTTA WITH WALNUTS AND HONEY

Asparagus is one of the few vegetables that remains true to its
season—though you can buy it earlier than ever, and it stays
around later than ever, it's still pretty much a spring vegetable.
Salmon, too, was once a symbol of spring; though it is no longer,
the combination still feels like an escape from winter.

KEYS TO SUCCESS

- You can use fillets of salmon (or any other sturdy fish) instead of steaks, and the results will be good. Broil on one side only, until the top is nicely browned and a thin-bladed knife passes to the bottom of the fillet without meeting much resistance.

- Fresh ricotta is not always easy to find; your best shot is at an Italian shop that makes it, or a good Italian grocery, or a swank cheese store. Good commercial ricotta is not a bad substitute.

- Pea-and-Ginger Soup (page 30) would also start this meal off nicely, and Strawberry Fool (page 51) would be a superb choice for dessert.

WINE

A light Pinot Noir (red Burgundy) or another fruity red, like Beaujolais; or a good Chardonnay (white Burgundy) or other sturdy white.

THE TIMETABLE

- The soup is definitely the first thing to do here, because it can be reheated at the last minute with almost no thought or effort.

- About 45 minutes before you're ready to eat, start the potatoes. When they're beginning to brown, reheat and serve the soup, keeping an eye on the potatoes.

- Finish the potatoes—once browned, they can be held hot over a very low flame while you prepare the salmon and beurre noisette.

- Make the ricotta dessert while you lasso someone else to clear the table and begin cleanup.

pan-roasted asparagus soup
with tarragon

You can save yourself some time by using thin asparagus; if you use thicker stalks, peel them first or the soup will be fibrous. Be especially careful whenever you puree hot liquid; do it in smaller batches to avoid spattering. (See page 158 for details.)

MAKES 8 SERVINGS

TIME: 40 MINUTES

3 pounds thin asparagus

1/4 cup (4 tablespoons) unsalted butter or extra virgin olive oil

20 fresh tarragon leaves, or 1 teaspoon dried

8 cups chicken or other stock

Salt and freshly ground black pepper

1. Break off the bottom part of each asparagus stalk and discard. Coarsely chop the rest of the stalks, leaving about twenty-five of the flower ends whole. Put the butter in a large, deep skillet or broad saucepan and turn the heat to medium-high. A minute later, add the asparagus and tarragon, raise the heat to high, and cook, stirring only occasionally, until nicely browned, about 10 minutes. Remove the whole flower ends; set aside.

2. Add the stock and some salt and pepper; bring to a boil, then reduce the heat and simmer until the asparagus is very tender, about 10 minutes. Cool for a few minutes.

3. Use a blender to carefully puree, in batches. Return to the pan, and, over medium-low heat, reheat gently, stirring occasionally. When the soup is hot, taste and adjust the seasoning. Put three to four of the cooked flower ends in each of eight bowls; ladle in the soup and serve.

broiled salmon with beurre noisette

Nothing like a little butter to jazz up a simple dish, and the complexity of browned butter—beurre noisette—really makes it happen.

MAKES 8 SERVINGS

TIME: 30 MINUTES

Eight 6-ounce salmon steaks (or use fillets of red snapper or other sturdy, white-fleshed fish)

Salt and freshly ground black pepper

8 tablespoons (1 stick) unsalted butter

2 tablespoons fresh lemon juice

Minced fresh parsley, chervil, dill, chives, or scallions, optional

1. Preheat the broiler, adjusting the rack so that it is 4 to 6 inches from the heat source. Sprinkle the salmon with salt and pepper. Broil until the first side is nicely browned, about 5 minutes; turn and cook just 2 or 3 minutes on the other side, or until the fish is done to your liking.

2. While the fish is cooking, put the butter in a small saucepan and turn the heat to medium. Cook, swirling the pan occasionally, until the butter stops foaming and begins to brown. Remove from the heat immediately and season lightly with salt and pepper; keep warm if necessary.

3. To serve, stir the lemon juice into the butter and drizzle a little of it over each piece of fish. Garnish if you like.

pan-crisped potatoes

The late, great Pierre Franey—author of The 60-Minute Gourmet—*showed me how to make these twenty years ago (of course he used butter), and I have been making them weekly ever since.*

MAKES 8 SERVINGS

TIME: 45 MINUTES

3 to 4 pounds waxy red or white potatoes, peeled and cut into $^1/_2$-inch to 1-inch cubes

$^1/_2$ cup olive oil, more or less

Salt and freshly ground black pepper

2 teaspoons minced garlic

1. Place the potatoes in a pot of salted water, bring to a boil, and simmer until nearly tender, 10 to 15 minutes. Drain well.

2. Heat the oil over medium-high heat in a 12-inch nonstick skillet for 3 or 4 minutes. You can use more oil for crisper potatoes, or less oil to cut the fat. (You can also use butter if you prefer, or a combination.) Add the potatoes along with a healthy sprinkling of salt and pepper, and cook, tossing and stirring from time to time (not constantly), until they are nicely browned all over, 10 to 20 minutes.

3. Add the garlic and continue to cook 5 more minutes, stirring frequently. Taste and adjust the seasoning if necessary, and serve.

ricotta with walnuts and honey

A traditional Mediterranean dessert. To toast the walnuts, either roast them in a 350°F oven or put them in a dry skillet over medium heat and cook, shaking the pan occasionally; in either case, they're done when they become fragrant or just begin to brown.

MAKES 8 SERVINGS

TIME: 10 MINUTES

4 cups fresh, moist ricotta

1 cup heavy cream or crème fraîche

1/2 cup sugar

2 cups toasted walnuts, broken into pieces

Honey to taste

Use a wooden spoon to beat together the ricotta, cream, and sugar until lightened. Scoop into eight bowls, top with walnuts, and drizzle with honey.

a family-style dinner

CABBAGE SOUP WITH APPLES

OVEN-"GRILLED" STEAK

PORCINI-SCENTED "WILD" MUSHROOM SAUTÉ (PAGE 218)

FAST POTATO GRATIN (PAGE 231)

BLUEBERRIES WITH SWEDISH CREAM

This is bistro-type food and a fitting launch to spring,
beginning with the fresh-tasting cabbage soup and continuing
with the steak (which will set you straight when you're
dying for some grilled food, but it's just too early) and
mushrooms. The potato gratin is bound to become a standard
part of your repertoire.

KEYS TO SUCCESS

- Sirloin strip or rib-eye are the best steaks for this style of cooking; either should be about an inch thick.

- A salad or steamed vegetable would make the meal somewhat more elaborate, but I don't think either is necessary.

WINE

Red, and good; a cru bourgeois from Bordeaux would be ideal—or any red wine with some body.

THE TIMETABLE

- Make the soup first and keep it warm (don't add the apples until the last minute). Prepare the ingredients for the other dishes.

- Next comes the gratin, which can come out of the oven when the steaks go in (cover it with foil and keep it in a warm place; it will be fine). Serve the soup.

- When the soup bowls are cleared, sauté the mushrooms and keep them warm, then make the steaks.

- Prepare the dessert, which takes just a few minutes, after eating the main course.

cabbage soup
with apples

This is a cabbage soup with a difference; the apples add sweetness, crunch, and complexity.

MAKES 8 SERVINGS

TIME: 40 MINUTES

2 tablespoons olive oil

4 tablespoons unsalted butter

2 large onions, sliced

2 pounds cabbage (weighed after trimming), shredded

20 thyme sprigs

Salt and freshly ground black pepper

10 cups chicken or beef stock

5 Golden Delicious or other good apples, peeled and cubed

1. In a medium saucepan, combine the oil and 1 tablespoon of the butter and turn the heat to medium-high. When the butter melts, add the onions and cabbage and cook, stirring occasionally, until the onions and cabbage wilt and begin to brown; add fifteen of the thyme sprigs and cook a few minutes more. Sprinkle with salt and pepper.

2. Add the stock and turn the heat to medium; stir occasionally as it heats. Put the remaining butter in a skillet and turn the heat to medium-high. When the butter foam subsides, add the apple pieces. Cook, stirring occasionally, until they brown and become tender, about 10 minutes. Strip the leaves from the remaining thyme sprigs and sprinkle them over the apples, along with a bit of salt.

3. Taste the soup and adjust the seasoning; remove the thyme sprigs. Serve the soup hot, garnished with the apple cubes.

oven-"grilled" steak

A minimalist preparation if ever there was one, this technique will put a great crust on your steaks.

MAKES 8 SERVINGS

TIME: 30 MINUTES

3 to 4 pounds sirloin strip or rib-eye steaks (4 large steaks should do it)

Salt and freshly ground black pepper

1. Preheat the oven to its maximum, 500°F or more, for at least 20 minutes; if it is equipped with a pizza stone, so much the better. About 10 minutes before you're ready to eat, put a cast-iron or other heavy ovenproof skillet large enough to hold the steaks on the stove over high heat. (If you must use two skillets, that's okay.) Wait 2 or 3 minutes, until the pan is beginning to smoke.

2. Add the steaks and let them sit on top of the stove as long as you can before the smoke becomes intolerable—probably no more than a minute. Immediately transfer the pan to the oven. Roast the steaks until nicely browned on the bottom, about 4 minutes, then turn and cook on the other side until done, another 3 or 4 minutes. Sprinkle with salt and pepper and serve immediately.

blueberries with swedish cream

This mixture of heavy and sour cream is akin to crème fraîche, but I find it more delicious. It's a killer on blueberries.

MAKES 8 SERVINGS

TIME: 15 MINUTES

1^1/2 cups heavy cream

^{3}/4 cup sour cream

Sugar or honey to taste

2 quarts blueberries, washed and picked over

1. Whip the heavy cream until it holds soft peaks, then fold it into the sour cream; add sweetener to taste.

2. Place the berries in eight bowls or stemmed glasses and top with the cream.

an eclectic spring menu

PEA-AND-GINGER SOUP

SALT-CURED COD WITH ARUGULA SAUCE

PERSIAN RICE WITH POTATOES

SAUTÉED BANANAS

This menu uses seasonal ingredients in a couple of uncommon ways. The soup (for which much credit goes to the late South American chef Felipe Rojas-Lombardi) is a brilliant combination that I'm sure you and your guests will like as much as I do; the lightly cured fish with arugula sauce is also a real winner. The meal is rounded off by a couple of standards, neither of which is prepared as often as it deserves to be.

KEYS TO SUCCESS

■ If you can find thin-skinned, fresh ginger—not uncommon in spring— you'll find its taste both brighter and less harsh than the thicker-skinned variety.

■ Make sure to rinse the salt from the fish well; and add no other salt to the dish, except perhaps a pinch to the arugula sauce.

■ Pan-Roasted Asparagus Soup with Tarragon (page 18) would also start this meal off well.

WINE

With all these bold flavors, selecting a wine is challenging.
A straightforward white with a little body, like a Pinot Blanc,
might be best, but I wouldn't give it too much thought; almost
nothing white will be too far off.

THE TIMETABLE

■ Start the rice a couple of hours before you want to eat; it takes a while but also holds well over low heat.

■ The soup can be prepared well in advance, or you can make it while the rice is cooking and the fish is resting with the salt.

■ Reheat the soup and serve it, then cook the fish and make the sauce while your guests relax.

■ The bananas must be cooked at the last moment; they do not take long.

pea-and-ginger soup

Fresh peas are inestimably better than frozen for munching, but by the time you cook them and mix them with ginger, they have lost much of their advantage. If you can't find them, or deal with them—the shelling does take a while—by all means use frozen.

MAKES 8 SERVINGS

TIME: 30 MINUTES

4 cups fresh or frozen peas

$^1/_4$ cup peeled and roughly chopped ginger (or more to taste, up to $^1/_2$ cup)

Salt and freshly ground black pepper

8 cups chicken or other stock

1. Combine all the ingredients in a saucepan and bring to a boil over medium-high heat. Reduce the heat to a simmer and cook until the peas and ginger are very tender, about 15 minutes. Cool for a few minutes.

2. Pour into a blender and carefully blend until pureed. (See the headnote on page 158.) Return to the pan, and, over medium-low heat, reheat gently, stirring occasionally. When the soup is hot, taste and adjust the seasoning and serve.

salt-cured cod with arugula sauce

Briefly salting fresh cod (or other delicate fish, like haddock, whiting, or sea trout) changes its texture slightly, and for the better: By removing just enough water to tighten the fillet's flesh, the salt enables you to poach the fish without worrying that it will fall apart.

MAKES 8 SERVINGS

TIME: 1 1/2 HOURS, LARGELY UNATTENDED

Coarse salt as needed

3 to 4 pounds thick-cut cod fillet

2 bay leaves

4 to 5 cups milk, fish stock, or water

4 cups washed arugula or watercress (thin stems are okay)

8 scallions, trimmed

1. On a plate or tray large enough to hold the fish in one layer, sprinkle salt to a depth of about 1/8 inch. Lay the cod on it and cover it with another layer of salt. Let stand for about 45 minutes.

2. Rinse the fish well, so that no traces of salt remain. Put it in a pan just large enough to hold it in one layer, and add the bay leaves and enough milk to barely cover. Bring to a boil over high heat, then adjust the heat so the mixture simmers gently. The fish is done when a skewer or thin-bladed knife passes through it with little resistance, 5 to 10 minutes.

3. Meanwhile, combine the arugula and scallions in a blender with a small pinch of salt and some of the poaching liquid. Blend until creamy, adding a little more liquid if necessary. When the fish is done, drain it, remove and discard the bay leaves, and serve the cod with the sauce.

persian rice
with potatoes

A perfect side dish for the lean fish. Skimp on the butter if you like, but the potatoes will not be as crisp or delicious. Better, I think, to switch to olive oil.

MAKES 8 SERVINGS

TIME: ABOUT 2 HOURS, LARGELY
UNATTENDED

2 cups good long-grain rice, like basmati

4 to 6 tablespoons unsalted butter or extra virgin olive oil

1 pound russet or other all-purpose potatoes, peeled and thinly sliced

Salt and freshly ground black pepper

1. Bring a large pot of water to a boil and salt it; add the rice and cook, stirring occasionally, as you would pasta. When it is nearly done, drain it.

2. While the rice is cooking, heat 2 tablespoons of the butter over medium heat in a wide skillet or casserole, preferably nonstick. Arrange the potatoes in the butter and sprinkle with salt and pepper. When the rice is done, pour it over the potatoes and turn the heat to very low. Add 2 more tablespoons of butter and cover. Cook over the lowest possible heat, undisturbed, for at least 1^1/2 hours, or until the potatoes are crisp (use a thin spatula to lift a bit of the mixture and peek). At this point you can hold it over minimum heat for another half hour or so, or turn off the heat, then reheat over medium-low heat for 15 minutes before serving. For extra richness, add another 2 tablespoons of butter, cut up, to the rice during the last few minutes of cooking. Serve hot.

sautéed bananas

The ideal bananas for cooking are just ripe, yellow with barely any brown spots. Double this recipe if you want a more substantial dessert, or serve with vanilla ice cream.

MAKES 8 SMALL SERVINGS

TIME: 15 MINUTES

4 bananas, ripe but not too soft

3 tablespoons unsalted butter

Flour for dredging

2 tablespoons sugar, plus more to pass at the table

Fresh lemon juice

1. Peel the bananas, cut them in half crosswise, then lengthwise, so that each banana has been made into four pieces. Place the butter in a large, deep skillet over medium-high heat.

2. Dredge the banana pieces lightly in the flour, shaking them to remove the excess. When the butter foam subsides, add the pieces to the skillet. Cook, turning frequently, until they are golden and beginning to brown, about 10 minutes. Sprinkle with the 2 tablespoons sugar and cook 1 minute more.

3. Serve, passing additional sugar and lemon juice at the table.

a pan-asian dinner

"RISOTTO" WITH COCONUT MILK AND SEAFOOD

BROILED LAMB CHOPS WITH MINT CHUTNEY

HERBED GREEN SALAD WITH SOY VINAIGRETTE

PINEAPPLE-GINGER SORBET (PAGE 77)

This elaborate meal can be served as a buffet or a sit-down dinner; it will work fine either way. The food is full-flavored, robust, delicious, and unusual, yet none of it is difficult to prepare. As the season progresses, you can grill the lamb instead of broiling it.

KEYS TO SUCCESS

- Make sure to use short-grain rice for the risotto; it can be the relatively expensive Italian Arborio, or rice grown in Asia or the States.

- To make this meal a more elaborate feast, add Broiled Bluefish or Mackerel with Green Tea Salt (page 153) or Miso-Broiled Scallops (page 198).

WINE

A tricky one, because you want white for the risotto—a fruity
one, like Gewürztraminer or Riesling—but red, like Pinot Noir, for the
chops. If I were going with only one I would opt for red.

THE TIMETABLE

- Ready the salad greens and dressing first.

- Prepare the ingredients for the sorbet and refrigerate them while the risotto is cooking. When done serving the risotto, dress the salad and broil the lamb.

- Put the sorbet mixture in the ice cream machine during or just after eating the main course. Like most frozen desserts, it is at its best when eaten as soon as possible after it has been made.

"risotto" with coconut milk and seafood

The creaminess that is the ideal in a finished risotto is not always easy to achieve. And the peak of creaminess does not necessarily coincide with the rice being cooked to the correct degree (which is, most believe, just a shade shy of complete tenderness). A load of butter helps, but most home cooks are reluctant to add this. Coconut milk, however, adds not only distinctive flavor, depth, and a touch of sweetness to a risotto, it practically guarantees a creamy result.

MAKES 8 SERVINGS

TIME: 40 MINUTES

2 tablespoons vegetable oil

2 cups short-grain rice, such as Arborio

1 1/2 cups dry white wine

Two 14-ounce cans coconut milk

1 cup diced tomato (canned is fine; drain well), optional

1 pound peeled and diced shrimp

Salt

1/4 teaspoon cayenne, or to taste

1/2 cup minced fresh basil, cilantro, or scallions, optional

1. Put the oil in a 10-inch skillet, preferably nonstick, and turn the heat to medium-high. Add the rice and cook, stirring occasionally, until the rice glistens and sizzles, 2 to 3 minutes. Put a small pot of water (2 or 3 cups) on the stove to heat up.

2. Add the wine and let it boil away, stirring once or twice, until the mixture is just about dry. Add 1 cup of the hot water and repeat, stirring frequently. Add half the coconut milk and, once again, cook, stirring frequently, until it is just about gone. Add the remaining coconut milk and repeat.

3. At this point the rice should be nearly tender; if it is not, repeat the process with another 1/2 cup hot water, or more if necessary. Stir in the tomato, if using, shrimp, salt to taste, and cayenne and cook until the mixture is creamy and the rice is tender but not mushy. (If the rice is still too crunchy for your taste, stir in another 1/2 cup hot water and cook, stirring, until the mixture is creamy again.) Garnish with the basil, if you like, and serve.

broiled lamb chops with mint chutney

Asparagus may introduce spring, but mint screams it. The perennial herb is among the first edible greens out of the ground, and it's rampant enough to be considered a weed for those who aren't fond of it. Team it with lamb, and you have a model spring dish.

MAKES 8 SERVINGS

TIME: 30 MINUTES

Juice of 2 limes

1 garlic clove

One 1-inch-long piece of ginger, peeled and roughly chopped

1 fresh or dried chile, or to taste

1 cup whole-milk yogurt

1 tablespoon sugar

2 cups fresh mint leaves, washed, well dried, and chopped

Salt and freshly ground black pepper

8 shoulder lamb chops

1. Prepare a charcoal grill or preheat a gas grill or broiler; the fire should be moderately hot and the rack 4 to 6 inches from the heat source.

2. To make the chutney, combine the lime juice, garlic, ginger, chile, yogurt, and sugar in the container of a food processor or blender and puree. Stir in the mint by hand, then add salt and pepper to taste.

3. When the chutney is ready, grill the chops 3 to 4 minutes per side, by which time they will be medium-rare, or until they reach the desired degree of doneness. Serve the lamb chops hot, with the chutney.

herbed green salad with soy vinaigrette

A load of herbs and a strong vinaigrette make this salad special.

MAKES 8 SERVINGS

TIME: 20 MINUTES

2 cups assorted chopped mild fresh herbs, like parsley, dill, mint, basil, and/or chervil

$1/4$ cup minced fresh chives

1 teaspoon minced fresh tarragon, optional

12 cups mesclun or other greens

1 cup grapeseed or olive oil

$1/2$ cup fresh lemon juice, or to taste

$1/4$ cup soy sauce

Freshly ground black pepper

Salt, optional

1. Combine the herbs and greens; cover with a damp towel and refrigerate until ready to serve, not more than a couple of hours.

2. When you're ready to serve, whisk together the oil, lemon juice, soy sauce, and about $1/2$ teaspoon of pepper. Add salt if necessary (it may not be). Toss with the greens, and add more salt or lemon juice if necessary; serve immediately.

a tuscan-style meal

PASTA WITH DARK RED DUCK SAUCE

CAULIFLOWER WITH GARLIC AND ANCHOVY

BREAD

OLIVE OIL COOKIES WITH RED WINE AND ROSEMARY

This is a dark, rich menu with deep flavors. Though it takes some time to prepare (the sauce simmers for a while), it's also quite simple and extremely informal, a meal that would work well for a small gathering of friends and family, or provide the basis for a larger feast.

KEYS TO SUCCESS

- Duck legs are not sold in every supermarket so, if you're planning this meal, make sure you can get them. Ordering them in advance should work as a last resort.

- If you prefer slightly sweeter cookies, see Olive Oil Sugar Cookies (page 109).

- To turn this into a feast, add a substantial fish dish, like Roast Striped Bass with Tomatoes and Olives (page 139).

WINE

Dark and red: Something made with the Nebbiolo grape
(like Barolo or Barbaresco) would be ideal. For cooking, use something
less expensive, like a fairly standard Cabernet or Zinfandel.

THE TIMETABLE

- This is an easy one: Make the cookies whenever you like. The sauce must be begun a couple of hours before you eat, so you can even make the cookies while it's simmering.

- The cauliflower can be made an hour or so in advance, or at the last minute.

pasta with dark red duck sauce

Every visitor to Tuscany comes away with a love of this nearly brown sauce, which can be made with duck or similar quantities of rabbit, beef, or pork.

MAKES 8 SERVINGS

TIME: 2 HOURS OR MORE, LARGELY UNATTENDED

4 duck legs

1 large onion, chopped

3 cups dry red wine

One 28-ounce can plum tomatoes, drained and roughly chopped

Salt and freshly ground black pepper

1 pound cut pasta, such as penne

Freshly grated Pecorino Romano or Parmesan

1. Trim the visible fat from the duck legs, then lay them, skin side down, in a large skillet. Turn the heat to medium and, when the duck begins to sizzle, turn the heat to low and cover. Cook undisturbed for about an hour (check once to make sure the legs aren't burning and adjust the heat if necessary), by which time the skin should be golden brown. Turn, cover again, then cook until the duck is very tender, at least 30 minutes more.

2. Remove the duck and set aside; remove most but not all of the fat. Add the onion to the skillet and turn the heat to medium-high. Cook, stirring occasionally, until the onion is softened, about 5 minutes. Set a large pot of water to boil for the pasta and salt it.

3. Add the wine to the onion and raise the heat to high; cook until the liquid is reduced by about half, then add the tomatoes along with some salt and pepper and cook over medium-high heat, stirring occasionally, until the mixture is saucy, about 15 minutes. Taste and adjust the seasoning.

4. Meanwhile, shred the duck from the bone and add it to the sauce as it cooks. A few minutes after adding the tomatoes, cook the pasta. When it is tender but not mushy, drain it and serve it with the sauce, along with the cheese.

cauliflower with garlic and anchovy

Buy snow-white cauliflower with no brown spots; use broccoli or one of the hybrids (broccoflower, Romanesco cauliflower, and so on) if the cauliflower does not look good. This dish is just as good warm as it is hot.

MAKES 8 SERVINGS

TIME: ABOUT 30 MINUTES

1 large head cauliflower, at least 2 pounds, trimmed of green parts and cut or broken into florets

6 tablespoons extra virgin olive oil

5 to 10 anchovy fillets, to taste, chopped

1 tablespoon minced garlic

1 teaspoon crushed red pepper flakes, or to taste, optional

Minced fresh parsley leaves

1. Place the cauliflower in a steamer above an inch or two of boiling salted water. Cover and cook until it is just tender, about 10 minutes, then plunge into a bowl of ice water to stop the cooking.

2. Combine the oil, anchovies, garlic, and crushed red pepper, if you are using it, in a large, deep skillet and turn the heat to medium-low. Cook, stirring occasionally, until the anchovies begin to break up and the garlic begins to color, about 5 minutes.

3. Add the cauliflower and raise the heat to medium-high. Continue to cook, stirring, for about 5 minutes more, until the cauliflower is coated with the oil and heated through. Garnish with the parsley and serve hot or at room temperature.

olive oil cookies with red wine and rosemary

You need not use your best olive oil for these cookies; one labeled "pure" or even "light" will be okay. But extra virgin olive oil will make them more interesting.

MAKES ABOUT 4 DOZEN

TIME: 30 MINUTES

$2^1/_2$ cups all-purpose flour

$^1/_2$ teaspoon baking powder

Pinch of salt

$^1/_8$ teaspoon freshly ground black pepper

1 teaspoon minced fresh rosemary leaves, or $^1/_2$ teaspoon dried

$^3/_4$ cup sugar

2 eggs

$^1/_2$ cup olive oil

$^3/_4$ cup dry red wine, or a little more

1. Preheat the oven to 375°F. Combine the dry ingredients. Beat the eggs with the olive oil and wine. Use a rubber spatula to stir the liquid mix into the dry one, just until well combined; if the mixture is stiff, add a little more wine.

2. Drop by rounded teaspoons onto a lightly oiled cookie sheet and bake until lightly browned, 12 to 15 minutes. Cool a couple of minutes, then remove the cookies to a rack to cool further. Store in a covered tin for up to 3 days.

a mostly made-in-advance buffet

SEAFOOD SALAD

SALMON AND TOMATOES COOKED IN FOIL

BIG CHOPPED SALAD WITH VINAIGRETTE (PAGE 148)

BREAD PUDDING WITH SHIITAKE MUSHROOMS

STRAWBERRY FOOL

This is a sizable buffet, but one in which all of the food is quite light. If the weather turns fine, your guests can wander outside, and the food will contribute to the springlike atmosphere; but if it is cool and dreary, this homey meal will warm them right up.

KEYS TO SUCCESS

- Almost any mixture of cooked seafood will work with the salad, so don't go crazy trying to make it too exotic. Two or three different kinds of shellfish are ideal.

- The bread pudding should be removed from the oven when it still appears slightly underdone. Like most puddings, it will retain heat and therefore firm up just fine. Use good white bread—torn from a loaf, not presliced—and the pudding will be much better.

WINE

A big Chardonnay, like a well-oaked specimen
from northern California, or a good white Burgundy.

THE TIMETABLE

- The seafood salad can be made a day in advance and will not suffer for it. Keep it refrigerated, of course, but bring it back to room temperature before serving; it should not be ice-cold.

- The salmon packages can also be assembled hours ahead of time. About 2 hours before you want to eat, start the bread pudding; while it's in the oven, attend to other tasks. Put the salmon in the oven after you remove the bread pudding and in any case no sooner than when you serve the seafood.

- Do the chopping for the salad early, but assemble it late.

- Make the puree for the fool in advance if you like, but do the rest of the work when you're ready for dessert.

seafood salad

To cook the seafood for this salad, just poach it in an inch or two of water; cover the pot, and the fish need not even be covered by the liquid. At the end you will have a decent fish stock for chowder or risotto.

MAKES 8 SERVINGS

TIME: 15 MINUTES

2 pounds cooked shrimp, lobster, crabs, conch, mussels, clams, octopus, and/or squid

$1/2$ cup minced fresh parsley

2 tablespoons capers

1 small garlic clove, finely minced

$1/2$ cup extra virgin olive oil

Salt and freshly ground black pepper

Fresh lemon juice to taste

1. Toss the seafood with the parsley, capers, garlic, all but a tablespoon of the olive oil, salt, pepper, and a couple of tablespoons of lemon juice.

2. Taste and add additional lemon juice if necessary. Drizzle with the remaining olive oil and serve.

salmon and tomatoes cooked in foil

Cooking in packages requires a small leap of faith to determine that the food is done, because once you open the packages you want to serve them. This method works well.

MAKES 8 SERVINGS (4 PACKAGES)

TIME: 40 MINUTES

8 tablespoons extra virgin olive oil

3 to 4 pounds salmon fillet, cut crosswise (8 pieces)

12 cherry tomatoes, sliced in half

Salt and freshly ground black pepper

32 fresh basil leaves

1. Put a baking pan in the oven and preheat it to 450°F. Take eight sheets of aluminum foil, each about 18 inches long, and place one piece on top of another to make four double sheets. Smear the bottom of each with 1 tablespoon of olive oil, then cover with two pieces of salmon, six tomato halves, some salt and pepper, eight basil leaves, and another tablespoon of oil. Fold the foil onto itself and crimp the edges as tightly as possible. Repeat the process. (You can refrigerate the packages until you're ready to cook, no more than 6 hours later.)

2. Put the packages in the baking dish and bake for about 15 minutes (or about 8 minutes from the time the package starts sizzling). Let sit for a couple of minutes before carefully slitting open each package and serving.

bread pudding
with shiitake mushrooms

This bread casserole is a major upgrade from stuffing.

MAKES 8 SERVINGS

TIME: ABOUT 1 HOUR, LARGELY
UNATTENDED

Butter or oil for the dish

8 ounces good white bread, cut or torn into chunks no smaller than 1 inch in diameter

2 cups milk

4 eggs

Salt and freshly ground black pepper

2 ounces freshly grated Parmesan

4 ounces freshly grated Emmentaler or other semisoft cheese

2 tablespoons unsalted butter or extra virgin olive oil

1 cup sliced shiitake mushrooms (caps only; stems should be reserved for stock or discarded)

1 teaspoon fresh thyme leaves, or $1/4$ teaspoon dried

1. Butter or oil an 8-inch soufflé or baking dish and put the bread in it. Combine the milk, eggs, salt, pepper, and cheeses and pour this mixture over the bread. Submerge the bread with a weighted plate and turn the oven to 350°F. Meanwhile, heat the butter or oil in a skillet over medium-high heat and sauté the mushrooms, stirring occasionally, until they begin to brown, about 10 minutes. Sprinkle them with additional salt and pepper and stir them into the bread mixture.

2. Bake until the pudding is just set but not dry, 35 to 45 minutes. The top will be crusty and brown. Serve hot, warm, or at room temperature.

strawberry fool

A simple, super-rich, traditional dessert.

MAKES 8 SERVINGS

TIME: 20 MINUTES

4 cups strawberries, picked over and trimmed of stems

1 cup plus 1 tablespoon superfine or confectioners' sugar, or more if needed

1 $1/2$ cups heavy cream, preferably not ultrapasteurized

1. Slice about two-thirds of the berries and toss them with $1/2$ cup sugar; set aside. Puree the remaining berries in a blender with another $1/2$ cup sugar. Force the puree through a sieve to remove the seeds. Taste; the puree should be quite sweet. If it is not, add a little more sugar.

2. Beat the cream with 1 tablespoon sugar, until it holds soft peaks. Stir in the puree, then fold in the sugared berries. Taste and add more sugar if necessary. Serve immediately or refrigerate for up to an hour.

an asian buffet

SLOW-COOKED RIBS WITH BLACK BEANS

CRISP PAN-FRIED NOODLE CAKE

STIR-FRIED LEEKS WITH GINGER AND SHRIMP

LIME GRANITA

Here is an unusual menu of mostly Chinese-style dishes—granita certainly doesn't qualify, but the lime flavor does—that makes a nice little buffet. The ribs and leeks are both fabulous, but if your guests are like mine, it will be the noodle cake that steals the show.

KEYS TO SUCCESS

- Cutting the ribs into short lengths will make it much easier for your guests to eat them, even if you don't choose to serve this meal buffet-style. Mirin (sweet rice wine) and fermented black beans can be purchased at any Asian market.

- The best noodles for the cake are fresh egg noodles, also sold at Asian markets, but you can use ordinary dried pasta if that's all you have.

- To expand this buffet, add Herbed Green Salad with Soy Vinaigrette (page 38) and/or Broiled Cornish Hens with Spicy Salt (page 210).

WINE

Beer would be preferable, but if you insist on wine, try a Gewürztraminer. Champagne is always suitable, too.

THE TIMETABLE

- Start the granita and the ribs at the same time. Prepare the leeks.

- If you're making two noodle cakes (which I recommend if you have more than six people), they'll take a while and require two pans, so get an early start on them.

- Keep the ribs warm while you finish the noodle cake and stir-fry the leek dish; then serve everything at once, remembering to stir the granita as necessary.

slow-cooked ribs
with black beans

The sauce from these ribs is fabulous with the noodle cake.

MAKES 8 SERVINGS

TIME: ABOUT 1½ HOURS

7 or 8 pounds spareribs, cut into
2-inch sections

2 star anise

½ cup dark soy sauce

1 cinnamon stick, about 3 inches
long

½ cup mirin, or ¼ cup honey
mixed with ¼ cup water

2 tablespoons sugar

2 tablespoons dry fermented
black beans

1 cup dry sherry

Minced cilantro, optional

1. Place the spareribs in a large skillet in one layer. Add the remaining ingredients except for the sherry and cilantro, along with 1 cup of water, and bring to a boil. Turn the heat to low, cover, and cook slowly— the mixture should bubble, but only gently—for at least an hour, turning the ribs every 20 minutes or so and adding additional water if necessary to keep the meat from drying out.

2. When the ribs are done—the meat will be tender and practically falling off the bone—remove them to a warm platter. Pour off most of the fat and turn the heat to high; add the sherry (if you don't have it, water will do) and cook, scraping up any brown bits on the bottom of the pan, until the liquid is reduced by about half, about 15 minutes. Serve the ribs, with this sauce, over rice or Crisp Pan-Fried Noodle Cake (page 55). Garnish with cilantro, if you like.

crisp pan-fried noodle cake

This recipe makes one noodle cake, which can be stretched to serve 8; but I recommend making two. You can prepare everything in one bowl, but cook the two cakes separately.

MAKES 1 CAKE

TIME: 30 MINUTES

12 ounces fresh egg noodles, or 8 ounces dried pasta

1/4 cup minced scallions

1 tablespoon soy sauce

4 tablespoons peanut (preferred) or other oil, plus more if needed

1. Cook the noodles in boiling salted water until tender but not mushy. Drain, then rinse in cold water for a minute or two. Toss with the scallions, soy sauce, and 1 tablespoon of the oil.

2. Place the remaining oil on the bottom of a heavy medium to large skillet, preferably nonstick; turn the heat to medium-high. When the oil is hot, add the noodle mix, spreading it out evenly and pressing it down.

3. Cook 2 minutes, then turn the heat to medium-low. Continue to cook until the cake is holding together and is nicely browned on the bottom. Turn carefully (the easiest way to do this is to slide the cake out onto a plate, cover it with another plate, invert the plates, and slide the cake back into the skillet, browned side up), adding a little more oil if necessary.

4. Cook on the other side until brown and serve.

stir-fried leeks with ginger and shrimp

Leeks, one of the first legitimate spring vegetables, are the highlight here (in fact this recipe is great without the shrimp; see page 211). In place of the shrimp, you could use scallops, tofu, chunks of chicken or pork, or slices of beef.

MAKES 8 SERVINGS

TIME: 30 MINUTES

$^1/_4$ cup peanut or olive oil

4 large leeks, about 3 pounds, cleaned and chopped (see page 211)

$1^1/_2$ to 2 pounds peeled shrimp

$^1/_4$ cup minced ginger

Salt and freshly ground black pepper

1 tablespoon good stock, dry sherry, or soy sauce, optional

1. Put half the oil in a large skillet, preferably non-stick, and turn the heat to high. When a bit of smoke appears, add the leeks, all at once. Let sit undisturbed for a couple of minutes, then cook, stirring only occasionally, for about 10 minutes. When the leeks dry out and begin to brown, remove them from the pan and set aside.

2. With the heat still on high, add the remaining oil to the pan, immediately followed by the shrimp; sprinkle with the ginger. Cook for about a minute; stir. Cook, stirring every minute or so, until the shrimp are almost all pink. Add the leeks, along with some salt and pepper. When the shrimp are done (no traces of gray will remain), stir in the liquid, if desired, taste and adjust the seasoning, and serve.

lime granita

Unlike almost every other frozen dessert, granitas take no special equipment. They do take some time, however, and do not keep well, so timing is important. Figure 2 to 3 hours for this, start to finish.

MAKES 8 SERVINGS

TIME: AT LEAST 2 HOURS, LARGELY UNATTENDED

1^{1}/4 cups sugar, or to taste

2 tablespoons minced or grated lime zest

2 cups fresh lime juice

1. Mix the sugar with 1^{1}/4 cups of boiling water and stir to dissolve. Add a cup of cold water and combine with the lime zest and juice. Taste and add more sugar if necessary.

2. Pour the prepared mixture into a shallow metal or glass pan or bowl. Freeze for about 30 minutes, or until ice crystals begin to form at the edges. Gently stir the crystals back into the liquid, not breaking them up entirely; a large fork is a good tool for this task.

3. Continue to stir and break up clumps of crystals every half hour or so. When the entire mixture has the texture of soft crushed ice, it's ready to serve. Serve immediately, or continue to stir every half hour or so until ready to serve. If the mixture becomes too hard, put it in a food processor for a few pulses, but do not puree; the consistency should not be too smooth.

the indoor clambake: an anticipation of summer

CLAMBAKE IN A POT

HERBED GREEN SALAD WITH NUT VINAIGRETTE

SUGARED STRAWBERRIES

Few preparations are more involved, or more challenging
(how many recipes begin with "build a wood fire on
a beach"?) than an outdoor clambake. But you can make a really
good one in a pot in your kitchen, and there is no better
way to celebrate the coming of summer.

KEYS TO SUCCESS

- If you want meat, which is a traditional part of a clambake, use kielbasa or linguiça, along with a piece of good, smoky slab bacon.

- The part of a clambake that takes longest to cook is the potatoes; you can shorten the cooking time considerably by using very small ones.

WINE

A chilled rosé from Provence or, if you can find it,
dry white (which is really pink) Zinfandel. A good sturdy
Chardonnay would not be out of place here either.

THE TIMETABLE

- Pretty straightforward; while the clambake is cooking, put together the salad and sugar the berries. Dress the salad just before serving.

clambake in a pot

Three or four ingredients are traditional in a clambake: clams (which should be littlenecks, not steamers, in order to minimize sandiness and making eating easier); lobster, of which you don't need much, about half per person; corn, an ear (or two, if it's good) per person; sausage, which you can certainly do without if you prefer; and melted butter, which is entirely optional. If you have those things, all you need to do, basically, is dump them in a pot, cover it, and turn on the heat. No kidding.

MAKES 8 SERVINGS

TIME: 45 MINUTES

1 to 2 pounds kielbasa, optional

1 to 2 pounds good slab bacon, in 2 pieces, optional

6 pounds hard-shell clams, washed

6 pounds mussels, washed and debearded

About 2 pounds tiny new potatoes, or any waxy potatoes, cut into chunks of less than 1 inch

Four $1^1/4$- to $1^1/2$-pound lobsters

8 ears corn, shucked

Melted unsalted butter, optional

1. Put the meat in the bottom of a very large pot, like a lobster pot (or use two large pots; just divide the ingredients in half). Add the clams and mussels, then the potatoes. Top with the lobsters and corn and add $1/2$ cup water. Cover and turn the heat to high.

2. Cook, shaking the pot a little every few minutes, for about 20 minutes. Remove the lid and carefully (there is a danger of scalding) check one of the potatoes to see whether it is tender. If not, re-cover and cook another 10 minutes or so.

3. Put the corn, meat, and lobsters on one or more platters (cut the lobsters in half). Put the mollusks in a large bowl and ladle some of the cooking juices over them. (Any clams that remain closed can be pried open with a dull knife.) Serve, if you like, with melted butter.

herbed green salad with nut vinaigrette

This dressing is not exactly a vinaigrette, since you just toss the oil and some vinegar or lemon juice on the greens. But it does the job beautifully.

MAKES 8 SERVINGS

TIME: 20 MINUTES

2 cups assorted chopped mild fresh herbs, like parsley, dill, mint, basil, and/or chervil

1/4 cup minced fresh chives

1 teaspoon minced fresh tarragon, optional

12 cups mesclun or other greens

Salt and freshly ground black pepper

1 cup hazelnut or walnut oil

Sherry vinegar or fresh lemon juice to taste

1. Combine the herbs and greens; cover with a damp towel and refrigerate until ready to serve, not more than a couple of hours.

2. When you're ready to serve, toss the greens with salt, pepper, and the oil. Add vinegar or lemon juice a tablespoon or two at a time, tasting until you are satisfied with the acidity. Add more salt and pepper if necessary and serve.

sugared strawberries

Look for strawberries that are dark red, inside and out. The sugar will juice up any strawberries, and make them sweeter of course, but it cannot work miracles.

MAKES 8 SERVINGS

TIME: 30 MINUTES

2 quarts strawberries, rinsed, hulled, and sliced

1/2 cup sugar, or more to taste

Sweetened whipped cream or vanilla ice cream, optional

Toss the strawberries with the sugar and let sit at room temperature for about 20 minutes, or until juicy. Serve, if you like, with whipped or ice cream.

summer

a spanish summer evening

MARINATED OLIVES

JEAN-GEORGES'S TOMATO-MELON GAZPACHO

GRILLED SWORDFISH "SANDWICH" WITH GREEN SAUCE

SIMPLE GREEN SALAD

POACHED CHERRIES

Here's a summer menu with a Spanish theme, one in which
all but the main course and the salad can be prepared in
advance. The flavors are lively, unusual (especially the gazpacho,
which has little in common with the standard variety),
and broadly appealing.

KEYS TO SUCCESS

- This wonderfully different gazpacho is so simple that the quality of ingredients becomes of paramount importance; the tomatoes and melon, especially, should be perfectly ripe.

- If you can find sour cherries for the dessert, they are ideal; if not, use firm Bing cherries.

- When you buy the swordfish, make sure it's a thick slice—an inch and a half is about right—and still has its skin on. This will make for a perfect "sandwich."

WINE

If you can lay your hands on an Albariño—the dry, slightly fruity, mildly spicy white from Galicia, in northwestern Spain—you will have a match made in heaven. Otherwise, any other white with some substance will do fine.

THE TIMETABLE

- You can prepare the olives days in advance, and they will be all the better for it.

- The gazpacho is a fresh dish, but it can sit in the refrigerator for the better part of a day without suffering any loss in quality. Same with the cherries.

- The green sauce can be made a couple of hours in advance, and you can even "stuff" the swordfish an hour or two in advance; refrigerate it until you're ready to cook. As always, you can also wash and dry the salad greens a couple of hours before eating.

marinated olives

An assortment of olives is far preferable to just one kind. Try, for example, some oil-cured, some big fat green Sicilians, and some Kalamatas—just that simple combination will look bright and pretty. If you can lay your hands on more varieties, so much the better.

MAKES 8 SERVINGS

TIME: 1 HOUR, LARGELY UNATTENDED

4 cups assorted olives

8 garlic cloves, lightly crushed

$^1/_4$ cup extra virgin olive oil

2 teaspoons fresh rosemary leaves

1 lemon, cut in half and segmented as you would a grapefruit

1. Toss together all the ingredients in a bowl. Marinate for an hour or longer at room temperature.

2. After the first day, refrigerate, then remove from the refrigerator an hour or two before serving.

jean-georges's tomato-melon gazpacho

You can turn this unusual gazpacho into a main course by adding some grilled shrimp or chicken to it.

MAKES 8 SERVINGS

TIME: 20 MINUTES, PLUS TIME TO COOL

8 tomatoes, about 3 pounds

Two 3-pound cantaloupes or other melon

$1/4$ cup olive oil

20 fresh basil leaves

Salt and freshly ground black pepper

Juice of 2 lemons

1. Core, peel, and seed the tomatoes; cut the flesh into 1-inch chunks. Seed the melon, and remove the flesh from the rind; cut into chunks. Place 2 tablespoons of olive oil in each of two large skillets and turn the heat under both to high (you can do this sequentially if you prefer). Add the melon to one and the tomatoes to the other and cook, stirring, until they both become juicy, about 3 minutes.

2. Divide the melon, tomatoes, and basil into two batches. Blend each with $1^1/2$ cups water and $^1/2$ cup ice cubes; season with salt and pepper. Chill, then add the lemon juice to taste and adjust the seasoning. Serve.

grilled swordfish "sandwich" with green sauce

Because the sauce is so moist, swordfish treated in this way will take a little longer to grill than usual; the interior, after all, has what amounts to a thick liquid cooling it off. So instead of cooking a 1 1/2-inch-thick steak—about the right size for this procedure—for 8 to 10 minutes, I'd estimate 12 to 14. The actual time will vary depending on the heat of your grill or broiler, but you can assume a little bit longer than what you're used to. Check by cutting into the fish when you think it's done; the interior can be pearly but should not look raw.

MAKES 8 SERVINGS

TIME: 30 MINUTES

20 anchovy fillets

3 cups fresh parsley leaves, washed and left wet

4 garlic cloves

Zest and juice of 2 lemons

1/2 cup extra virgin olive oil, or more if needed

1/4 cup capers, with their liquid

2 large swordfish steaks, skin on (about 3 to 4 pounds total)

Salt and freshly ground black pepper

1. Prepare a charcoal grill or preheat a gas grill or broiler; the fire should be moderately hot and the rack 4 to 6 inches from the heat source. Combine the anchovies, parsley, garlic, zest and lemon juice, and 2 tablespoons of the oil in a small food processor or blender. Process until pureed, adding a little bit of hot water (or more olive oil) if necessary to allow the machine to do its work. Combine the puree with the capers.

2. Cut the swordfish in half horizontally, leaving the skin attached as a hinge. Spread about a quarter of the green sauce on the inside of each "sandwich," then close the steak with a couple of toothpicks. Brush with the remaining oil, then sprinkle with the salt and pepper.

3. Grill at least 5 minutes per side, or until the swordfish is done (it should remain slightly translucent in the center). Cut the swordfish into slices or wedges and serve with the remaining green sauce.

simple green salad

Many people are hooked on premade salad dressing because they believe that homemade dressing is a production, but it need not be. Try this.

MAKES 8 SERVINGS

TIME: 10 MINUTES

About 12 cups torn assorted greens (trimmed, washed, and dried)

$1/2$ cup extra virgin olive oil, more or less

$1/4$ cup balsamic vinegar or sherry vinegar, or fresh lemon juice to taste

Pinch of salt, plus more to taste

Freshly ground black pepper to taste, optional

Place the greens in a bowl and drizzle them with the oil, vinegar, and a pinch of salt. Toss and taste. Correct the seasoning, add pepper, if desired, and serve immediately.

poached cherries

Sour cherries are too acidic to eat raw, but are the best for cooking. This simple preparation amounts to cherry pie without the crust. Like pie, they're great with vanilla ice cream.

MAKES 8 SERVINGS

TIME: ABOUT 30 MINUTES

3 to 4 pounds cherries, preferably sour

1 cup sugar, or more to taste

1/2 teaspoon ground cinnamon, optional

Fresh lemon juice, if using sweet cherries, to taste

1. Pit the cherries and combine them with 1 cup water in a medium saucepan; turn the heat to medium-high and cook, stirring occasionally, until the cherries are very tender, about 20 minutes.

2. Stir in the sugar and the cinnamon, if you are using it; taste and add more sugar or some lemon juice, if you like. Cool, then chill and serve the cherries cold, with their juice.

grilling, asian-style

❧

Here is a menu built around the grilled, hot-weather food of another continent. The shrimp is a kind of cocktail, though the only thing it has in common with the usual shrimp cocktail is the shrimp. The steak has an unusual, strong-flavored sauce that anyone who likes Thai food will enjoy, and grilled corn is a popular snack all over Southeast Asia. Finally, there is a tropical sorbet with a bit of a kick.

KEYS TO SUCCESS

- Skirt steak is an increasingly popular boneless steak that must be served rare or medium-rare, or it becomes tough. If someone insists on well-done meat, cut a piece off the steak and cook it separately. (It will not be very good.)

- Grilled corn is good with or without melted butter; it's best when some of the kernels are lightly charred.

- To make pineapple puree, take fresh (preferably) or canned pineapple and whiz it in a blender, with a tiny bit of pineapple juice or, if necessary, water, just enough to get the machine going. You'll need a little more than 4 cups pineapple chunks for this recipe.

- This menu is most easily and appropriately expanded by adding Herbed Green Salad with Soy Vinaigrette (page 38).

WINE

Given that this is likely to be an outdoor barbecue, I would go with beer. But an ice-cold rosé would be nice, too.

THE TIMETABLE

- Make the puree for the sorbet whenever you like and keep it cool; don't put it in the ice cream machine until you start eating, however—it will really be at its best straight from the machine.

- Make the sauces and shuck the corn while the grill preheats.

- Grill and eat the shrimp. Then grill and eat the steak and corn. Simple as that.

soy-dipped shrimp

Many people will find this their idea of paradise: simply grilled shrimp in a strong-flavored soy dipping sauce.

MAKES 8 SERVINGS

TIME: 40 MINUTES

2 tablespoons medium-hot paprika

$1/4$ cup peanut oil

Salt and freshly ground black pepper

3 pounds shrimp, peeled

1 cup good soy sauce

1 tablespoon minced garlic

1 tablespoon minced ginger

$1/4$ cup fresh lemon juice

$1/4$ teaspoon cayenne, or to taste

1. Start a grill fire. Mix the paprika, peanut oil, salt, and pepper, and rub all over the shrimp. When the fire is moderately hot, grill the shrimp, turning once, until done, about 5 minutes. Meanwhile, mix the soy sauce with the garlic, ginger, lemon juice, and cayenne; taste and adjust the seasoning as necessary.

2. Serve the shrimp hot, with the soy dipping sauce.

grilled skirt steak with thai-style sauce

Cooked medium-rare, skirt steak is juicy and as delicious as can be. Sauced, it's just incredible.

MAKES 8 SERVINGS

TIME: 40 MINUTES

1 garlic clove

1 small hot chile, stemmed and seeded, or more to taste

2 tablespoons sugar

1/2 cup fresh lime juice, or more to taste

1/3 cup nam pla (Thai fish sauce)

3 pounds skirt steak, in 2 pieces

Salt, if necessary

1/2 cup minced fresh mint leaves

1. Start a charcoal or gas grill; the fire should be quite hot, and the grill rack no more than 4 inches from the heat source. While it is heating, combine the garlic, chile, sugar, lime juice, and nam pla in a blender or small food processor and blend until nearly smooth; or mince the garlic and chile and combine them with the sugar, lime juice, and nam pla.

2. Grill the steak until medium-rare, about 3 minutes per side. Taste the sauce and adjust the seasoning if necessary, adding salt and more lime or chile if you like. Just before serving, stir in the mint. Serve the meat with the sauce on the side.

grilled corn

A real treat. If your fire is raging hot, remove the inner silks from the corn and grill them in their husks. But if it's in the normal range, grill the shucked corn directly over the fire. Ideally, some of the kernels will brown and even char.

MAKES 8 SERVINGS

TIME: 40 MINUTES

8 ears fresh corn

Melted unsalted butter, optional

Salt and freshly ground black pepper

1. Start a charcoal or wood fire, or preheat a gas grill. Shuck the corn.

2. Grill the corn, turning occasionally. When some of the kernels char a bit and others are lightly browned—5 to 15 minutes, depending on the heat of the grill—the corn is done. Brush with melted butter, if you like, and sprinkle with salt and pepper.

pineapple-ginger sorbet

A special combination, decidedly Asian. Use fresh ginger if at all possible.

MAKES 8 SERVINGS

TIME: 10 MINUTES, PLUS TIME TO

FREEZE THE MIXTURE

1 cup sugar

1 tablespoon very finely minced
fresh or candied ginger, or
1 teaspoon dried ginger, or to
taste

4 cups pineapple puree

Whisk the sugar and ginger into the puree and freeze in an ice cream machine, according to the manufacturer's directions. This is best when served straight from the machine, or after spending no more than an hour or two in the freezer.

a cool dinner for a hot night

COLD PEA SOUP

WATERMELON, THAI-STYLE

GRILLED CHICKEN, SAUSAGE, AND VEGETABLE SKEWERS

LEMON GRANITA

Aside from some quickly grilled skewers of chicken and vegetables—a kind of one-dish meal—this menu is entirely cool, and wonderful to eat outside on a hot night.

KEYS TO SUCCESS

- Unlike the pea soup on page 30, this one is unusual in that it uses the pods as well as the peas, so you can buy fresh peas without worrying about the hassle of shelling them.

- Chicken thighs are better for grilling than breasts, especially when boneless; they remain juicier and become tender instead of tough. If you cannot find boneless thighs in the supermarket, removing the meat from the bone is intuitive and fast. You can skewer the chicken and vegetables on branches of rosemary, if you have them; if not, use ordinary skewers and tuck some rosemary leaves in among the food.

- You don't expect smooth texture from a granita; that's not what it's about. The ideal granita is a slushy blend of juicy crystals in ice-cold liquid; don't let it get too hard.

WINE

A rough, assertive, but not too heavy red, like Chianti or something from the south of France.

THE TIMETABLE

- The soup can be made as far in advance as you like, up to a day or two.

- Start the granita at least a couple of hours before you want to eat it.

- The chicken and vegetables can be skewered a couple of hours ahead of time (in fact, I think they're better for it, as the rosemary flavor permeates everything); refrigerate until you're ready to grill.

cold pea soup

This soup is on the thin, almost drinkable, side, and if that doesn't appeal to you there are a couple of options I can recommend: One is to use a bit more sour cream than the quantity I recommend below. The other is to throw a peeled, diced potato in with the peas; this will give the final soup quite a bit of heft.

MAKES 8 SERVINGS

TIME: 30 MINUTES, PLUS TIME TO CHILL

2 pounds peas (in the shell), snow peas, or sugar snap peas (frozen are perfectly acceptable)

8 cups chicken or vegetable stock

Salt and freshly ground black pepper

$^1/_4$ cup heavy or sour cream, or more to taste

Chopped fresh parsley, optional

1. Combine the peas and stock in a saucepan and bring to a boil over medium-high heat. Reduce the heat to a simmer and cook until the peas are bright green and tender, 10 minutes or so. Cool for a few minutes. If you're using shell peas, remove some from their shells for garnish (refrigerate until serving). If you're using snow or snap peas, set a few aside.

2. Pour into a blender and carefully blend until pureed. (See the headnote on page 158.) Add salt and pepper to taste, then force through a fairly fine strainer, discarding the solids. Stir or whisk in the cream and refrigerate (up to 2 days) before serving, cold. Garnish with the reserved peas or some parsley, if you like.

watermelon, thai-style

A frequently seen snack in Bangkok and elsewhere in Southeast Asia.

MAKES 8 SERVINGS

TIME: 10 MINUTES

Eight 1-inch-thick wedges of watermelon

Salt, to pass at the table

Finely ground dried chiles, to pass at the table

Lime wedges, to pass at the table

Put the watermelon on plates and pass the remaining ingredients, allowing guests to season the melon to taste.

grilled chicken, sausage, and vegetable skewers

Branches of rosemary are ideal, because you can slide the food right onto them (in the direction of the needles, so as not to dislodge them), and they flavor it brilliantly; but so does some rosemary tucked in among the chunks of food. If you skewer on wood or metal skewers, turning will be made easier if you use two parallel sticks for each one, separating them by about $1/2$ inch; you can also buy two-pronged metal skewers that do the trick nicely.

MAKES 8 SERVINGS

TIME: 40 MINUTES

8 chicken thighs, boned and skinned, small thighs cut in half, larger ones in thirds or quarters

1 pound sweet or hot Italian sausage, cut into 1- to 2-inch lengths, optional

3 lemons, cut into eighths

$1^1/2$ pounds eggplant, zucchini, or baby pattypan squash, cut into 1-inch pieces

3 bell peppers, preferably red and yellow, cut into 2-inch sections

Salt and freshly ground black pepper

Several rosemary sprigs—or 8 branches

1. Start a gas or charcoal grill or preheat the broiler; the fire should be moderately hot. If you're using wooden skewers, soak them in water to cover while you prepare the food. Make 8 skewers, alternating the different ingredients but generally surrounding both the chicken and sausage with the moister lemons, eggplant, and peppers. Pack the food fairly tightly together on each skewer and sprinkle with salt and pepper. If you are not using rosemary skewers, tuck some rosemary in among the cubes of food.

2. Grill over moderate heat, covered or not, turning the skewers three or four times to brown evenly. Total cooking time will be 10 to 15 minutes, depending on the heat of the grill and the distance from the heat source to the rack. By the time the chicken and sausage are browned, the eggplant will be tender; do not overcook.

3. Remove the ingredients from the skewers and serve, squeezing hot lemon juice from the cooked lemons over all.

lemon granita

The more zest you include here, the better the flavor—I would consider this amount the minimum—but be careful to avoid the white, pithy part of the peel, which is bitter.

MAKES 8 SERVINGS

TIME: 15 MINUTES, PLUS TIME TO FREEZE

1^1/2 cups sugar, or to taste

2 tablespoons minced or grated lemon zest

2 cups fresh lemon juice

1. Mix the sugar with a cup of boiling water and stir to dissolve. Add another cup of cold water and combine with the citrus zest and juice. Taste and add more sugar if necessary.

2. Pour the prepared mixture into a shallow metal or glass pan or bowl. Freeze for about 30 minutes, or until ice crystals begin to form at the edges. Using a fork, gently scrape the crystals back into the liquid, not breaking them up entirely.

3. Continue to stir and break up clumps of crystals every half hour or so. When the entire mixture has the texture of soft crushed ice, it's ready to serve. Serve immediately, or continue to stir every half hour or so until ready to serve. If the mixture becomes too hard, put it in a food processor for a few pulses, but do not puree; the consistency should not be too smooth.

a mediterranean summer day

FENNEL WITH OLIVE OIL DIPPING SAUCE

MUSSEL AND POTATO SALAD

GRILLED FLANK STEAK WITH PROVENÇAL SPICES

EASY SUMMER PUDDING

Fennel, olive oil, mussels, rosemary, berries—all flavors that evoke the Mediterranean—are combined here in a pleasing menu for a summer day. All of these dishes are familiar enough, but each of these recipes has a novel twist that makes it unexpectedly delicious.

KEYS TO SUCCESS

- When cleaning mussels, discard any with broken shells. If the mussels have beards—the hairy vegetative growth that is attached to the shell—trim them off. Those mussels that remain closed after the majority have been steamed open can be pried open with a knife before adding their meat to the salad.

- If you don't have fresh lavender or rosemary, use dried, but cut the amounts in half. If you can't find lavender at all, increase the amounts of rosemary and thyme proportionally.

- Frozen pound cake is fine for the summer pudding (homemade is better, of course, but not one in ten people will taste the difference), but fresh berries are essential.

WINE

A sprightly red, like Beaujolais, or a lighter Côtes du Rhone, preferably chilled.

THE TIMETABLE

- Summer pudding must rest overnight—or for at least 6 hours—before serving. So, obviously, start with that.

- As far in advance as you can work, steam the mussels; then you can cool them and remove the meat from their shells at your leisure. You can then make the salad.

- Prepare the fennel and its sauce before starting the grill. Once the grill is going, you can make the rub for the meat.

fennel with olive oil dipping sauce

Fennel remains exotic enough to be a treat, and this simple preparation simply elevates its stature a bit.

MAKES 8 SERVINGS

TIME: 15 MINUTES

1/2 cup olive oil

1 garlic clove, peeled and lightly crushed

Salt and freshly ground black pepper

Minced zest of 1 lemon

1 fennel bulb, trimmed and cut into strips

1. Combine half the olive oil and garlic in a small saucepan and turn the heat to medium-low. Cook, shaking the pan occasionally, until the garlic begins to sizzle. Remove the garlic from the oil and the pan from the heat.

2. Add the remaining oil to the hot oil, along with the salt, pepper, and lemon zest. Serve as a dipping sauce with the fennel.

mussel and potato salad

My dressing of choice is a simple vinaigrette, here just oil and vinegar augmented by a handful each of chopped shallots for crunch and flavor and parsley for color and freshness. The result is a great summer dish, good-looking and good-tasting. As it stands, this is a potato salad with mussels; if you like, you can increase the amount of mussels, by as much as double, giving each component equal weight.

MAKES 8 SERVINGS

TIME: 45 MINUTES

4 pounds mussels, washed and debearded

2 pounds waxy new potatoes, cut into $1/2$-inch cubes

1 cup dry white wine or water

1 cup chopped shallots or red onion

1 cup extra virgin olive oil, or more if needed

$1/2$ cup balsamic or sherry vinegar

Salt and freshly ground black pepper

1 cup chopped fresh parsley, dill, chives, or a combination

1. Combine the mussels, potatoes, and wine in a broad, steep-sided skillet or casserole. Cover and turn the heat to high. When steam rises from the top, shake the pan once or twice and turn the heat to medium. Continue to cook until all the mussels open, checking after 5 minutes or so and then every couple of minutes. When the mussels are done, use tongs or a slotted spoon to remove them to a plate; leave the potatoes in the skillet and re-cover.

2. Cook until the potatoes are almost tender, then remove the cover and turn the heat to high, cooking until most of the liquid evaporates and the potatoes are done. By this time, the mussels will be cool enough to remove from their shells; do so, putting them in a large bowl.

3. When the potatoes are done, add them to the bowl with the mussels along with the shallots, oil, vinegar, salt, and pepper. Taste and adjust the seasoning as necessary. Serve immediately, an hour or two later, or cold, stirring in the herb(s) at the last moment.

grilled flank steak with provençal spices

Flank steak, more than most others, is tolerant of medium doneness, but in any case it must be sliced thinly, against the grain.

MAKES 8 SERVINGS

TIME: 30 MINUTES

5 tablespoons extra virgin olive oil

1 1/2 teaspoons salt

4 garlic cloves

1 tablespoon fresh rosemary leaves

1 tablespoon fresh lavender leaves

1 tablespoon fennel seeds

1 tablespoon fresh thyme leaves

2 teaspoons cracked black pepper

1 flank steak, about 3 pounds

1. Start a charcoal or wood fire or preheat a gas grill or the broiler. Combine all ingredients except the steak in a small food processor and blend until minced but not pureed (you can, of course, mince by hand). Rub all over the steak.

2. When the fire is hot, grill the steak about 4 minutes per side, or until nicely browned, for medium-rare, turning only once. Remove from the fire and let rest for about 5 minutes before slicing thinly and serving.

easy summer pudding

Substitute 1 cup of blueberries for $^1/_2$ cup of the raspberries if you like; stir them into the cooked raspberries while still hot.

MAKES 8 SERVINGS

TIME: 20 MINUTES, PLUS AT LEAST 6 HOURS FOR RESTING

3 pounds fresh or frozen raspberries

$^1/_2$ cup sugar, or to taste

$1^1/_2$ to 2 pounds pound cake

Lightly sweetened whipped cream, sour cream, or crème fraîche

1. Rinse the berries, then combine in a saucepan with the sugar and $^1/_4$ cup of water. Cook gently, stirring occasionally, just until the berries soften and yield their liquid, 10 to 15 minutes. Cool.

2. Meanwhile, cut the pound cake into roughly $^1/_2$-inch-thick slices. Line a rounded bowl with just over half the slices of the pound cake to a depth of about 4 inches; pack the slices so they leave no (significant) gaps. When the berries are cool, strain them, reserving the liquid. Spoon the solids on top of the pound cake and drizzle with about half the liquid.

3. Cover with the remaining slices of pound cake, again packing them close together. Drizzle with all but a few tablespoons of the remaining liquid (refrigerate the rest).

4. Find a plate that will just fit in the bowl, and press it down on top of the pudding. Weight it with a few cans (or whatever you can find that will do the trick) and refrigerate overnight, or for at least 6 hours.

5. To serve, run a knife around the edge of the pudding and invert onto a plate. Drizzle with the refrigerated liquid. Cut slices and serve with the cream.

a barbecue for meat lovers

SPICY GRILLED CHICKEN WING SALAD

GRILLED SOY-AND-GINGER BONELESS LEG OF LAMB

GRILLED FLATBREADS

GRILLED ZUCCHINI

EASY SUMMER PUDDING (PAGE 89) OR ICE CREAM

The double-meat whammy of this menu makes it a difficult barbecue for vegetarians (though the zucchini, flatbreads, and dessert might keep them happy). People who love crisp, juicy meat, however, will be ecstatic.

KEYS TO SUCCESS

- The best way to grill the chicken is over indirect heat, with a fire on one side, the wings on the other, and a cover on the grill; this practically eliminates the risk of burning. Once the wings are nearly done, you can move them to right above the coals (or flame, in the case of a gas grill) and crisp them up a bit. If you must grill over direct heat, make the fire moderate and keep a constant eye on things.

- The lamb can be grilled over direct or indirect heat; it, too, should be watched, though it is not as flammable as the chicken wings.

- Zucchini cooks quickly, and is good lightly browned and still somewhat crisp or fully cooked and tender. The flatbreads need to be grilled only until grill marks appear.

WINE

Red and rustic, like Zinfandel, Chianti, or lightly
chilled Beaujolais. A cool Provençal rosé wouldn't be bad either.

THE TIMETABLE

- If you're making the summer pudding, that must be begun at least 6 hours and preferably the day before. Otherwise, start with the lamb; it's good for it to sit with the spices rubbed into it for a while.

- Get the salad greens ready and grill the chicken wings; dress the salad, put the chicken on top, and serve it. This will hold people while you deal with the remaining courses (you can stop and eat, of course).

- Then grill the lamb until it is done; while it's resting, but before you carve it, grill the zucchini and the breads.

spicy grilled chicken wing salad

The fact that chicken wings are the cheapest cut of the bird in no way reflects their intrinsic value. After all, they have distinct advantages: You can grill them until they are crisp without drying out their interior; their high skin-to-meat ratio makes them especially delicious; and their meat is neither white nor dark, but both. (Furthermore, you can eat them with your hands.) It doesn't take much to build a delicious late-summer meal around them.

This recipe makes two wings per person; as a starter, that's sufficient. Double this recipe if you want to make the wings the main course and skip the lamb.

MAKES 8 SERVINGS

TIME: 45 MINUTES

$^1/_2$ cup extra virgin olive oil

10 garlic cloves

$^1/_2$ teaspoon cayenne, or to taste

Salt

16 chicken wings

$^1/_4$ cup sherry or other good vinegar, or to taste

6 cups torn romaine

Freshly ground black pepper

1. Prepare a charcoal grill or preheat a gas grill or broiler; the fire should be moderately hot and the rack 4 to 6 inches from the heat source. Put the olive oil in the narrowest saucepan you have and add the garlic. Turn the heat to medium-low and, when the garlic begins to sizzle, swirl the pan occasionally so the garlic rolls about a bit in the oil. When the garlic is lightly browned and tender (a thin-bladed knife will penetrate it easily), turn off the heat.

2. Combine 2 tablespoons of the oil with the cayenne and a big pinch of salt and toss the wings in this mixture. Grill, over indirect heat if possible, turning occasionally (and keeping an eye out for scorching), until the wings are crisp and cooked through, 20 to 40 minutes.

3. Meanwhile, once the oil has cooled, put it in a blender with the garlic, a pinch of salt, and the vine-

gar. Whiz until smooth; if it is too thick, add a little more oil, some hot water, or, if it is not strong enough for your taste, some more vinegar. Toss with the greens. Serve the salad with the chicken wings on top.

grilled soy-and-ginger boneless leg of lamb

Simply put, boneless lamb leg is the ideal meat for grilling. Not only is it full-flavored, it's completely forgiving; since its unusual shape virtually guarantees that some pieces will be well done while others remain rare, your guests will think you're a genius.

MAKES 8 SERVINGS

TIME: ABOUT 60 MINUTES

One 4-pound butterflied leg of lamb

1 tablespoon olive oil

2 teaspoons salt

1 teaspoon cracked black pepper

1 tablespoon minced garlic

1/4 cup soy sauce

1 tablespoon peeled and minced or grated ginger

Lemon wedges

1. Start a charcoal or wood fire or preheat a gas grill or broiler; the fire should be quite hot, and the rack should be at least 4 inches from the heat source. Trim the lamb of any excess fat. Mix together the olive oil, salt, pepper, garlic, soy, and ginger; rub this mixture into the lamb well, making sure to get some into all the crevices. (The lamb may sit, for an hour or more; refrigerate if it will be much longer.)

2. Grill or broil the meat until it is nicely browned, even a little charred, on both sides, 20 to 30 minutes, and the internal temperature at the thickest part is about 125°F; this will give you some lamb that is quite rare, as well as some that is nearly well done. Let rest for 5 minutes before slicing thinly, as you would a thick steak. Garnish with lemon wedges and serve.

grilled flatbreads

MAKES 8 SERVINGS

TIME: 15 MINUTES

8 to 16 small pita breads

Melted unsalted butter or extra
virgin olive oil, as needed

Start a moderately hot grill fire. Lightly brush the
breads with butter and grill, turning occasionally, until warm and lightly browned on each side.

grilled zucchini

8 SERVINGS

TIME: 20 MINUTES

3 pounds zucchini, washed

$1/4$ cup plus 2 tablespoons extra virgin olive oil

Salt and freshly ground black pepper

Chopped fresh parsley for garnish

1. Start a moderately hot grill fire. Cut the zucchini the long way into strips no more than $1/2$ inch thick. Rub all the strips with $1/4$ cup of olive oil and grill, turning once or twice, until nicely browned and tender, about 10 minutes.

2. Season with salt and pepper, garnish with the remaining olive oil and the parsley, and serve hot or at room temperature.

a meal for questionable weather

PASTA WITH GORGONZOLA AND ARUGULA

BROILED OR GRILLED SOFT-SHELL CRABS

GRILLED WHITE-AND-SWEET POTATO SALAD

CITRUS WITH HONEY AND MINT

Not every summer day is guaranteed to be sunny and hot, so here is a menu that allows you to cook indoors or out, depending on what happens. The pasta dish, of course, will be prepared on your stove, but both crabs and potato salad are equally good whether grilled or made in the broiler or oven.

KEYS TO SUCCESS

- If you can find larger arugula, it will be stronger-tasting and more distinctive than the young, tender leaves usually sold in supermarkets; I think this is a good thing. If you can't find Gorgonzola, use a good Roquefort or Stilton.

- Soft-shell crabs are almost always sold cleaned, but it's worth asking; you don't want to clean them yourself. Buy them no more than 24 hours before cooking them.

- Make sure you have good mustard—whole-grain or Dijon—for the potato salad; the bright yellow or even "spicy" brown will not cut it.

WINE

A dry white with some fruit: Chardonnay, Viognier, even—if you can find it—Vouvray or dry Chenin Blanc.

THE TIMETABLE

- Grill or roast the potatoes whenever you get a chance, even a day ahead of time.

- Make the dessert early in the day again, or up to a couple of days before serving.

- A half hour or so before you want to eat, start the pasta and serve it. The crabs are so quick to prepare that you can ready them in not much more than the time it takes to clear the pasta plates from the table.

pasta with gorgonzola and arugula

There are pasta sauces you can make in the time it takes the pasta-cooking water to come to the boil, and there are those that are really fast—those that can be made in the 8 to 10 minutes it takes to actually cook the pasta. This is one of the latter, one that boasts just a couple of main ingredients and a supporting cast of two staples.

MAKES 8 SERVINGS

TIME: 30 MINUTES

2 pounds cut pasta, like ziti or farfalle

4 tablespoons ($^1/2$ stick) unsalted butter

$^1/2$ pound ripe Gorgonzola

12 ounces arugula

Salt and freshly ground black pepper

1. Bring a large pot of water to a boil for the pasta. Meanwhile, melt the butter over low heat in a small saucepan; add the Gorgonzola and cook, stirring frequently, until the cheese melts. Keep warm while you cook the pasta.

2. Tear the arugula into bits, or use a scissors to cut it up—the pieces should not be too small. Cook the pasta until it is tender but not mushy. Remove and reserve a little of the cooking water, then drain the pasta and toss it with the arugula and the cheese mixture, adding a bit of the cooking water if the mixture seems dry.

3. Taste and adjust the seasoning—the dish should take plenty of black pepper—and serve.

broiled or grilled soft-shell crabs

Though you can just shove the crabs in the broiler, I find that this procedure works best: Preheat a large roasting pan in the broiler for 10 minutes or so. When you're ready to cook, put the crabs in the pan, adjusting the broiler rack so that it's 2 or 3 inches from the heat source, or as close as you can get it (in my oven, this means propping the roasting pan on top of another pan). The crabs will be done in less than 5 minutes. Remember that some oven broilers work best if the door is ajar, which will keep the element from cycling off and accelerate cooking time.

MAKES 8 SERVINGS

TIME: 15 MINUTES

8 soft-shell crabs

2 tablespoons extra virgin olive oil, optional

Salt

2 lemons, quartered

Melted unsalted butter, optional

1. Preheat the broiler, adjusting the rack so that it is just beneath the heat source; put a large nonstick roasting pan or skillet in there to heat up for about 10 minutes. Or start a grill, adjusting the rack so that it is about 4 inches from the coals.

2. To broil, place the crabs, top shell up, in the pan. Broil until they are firm and their tops are lightly browned, 3 to 5 minutes. Brush lightly with the olive oil, if you like. Sprinkle with salt, and serve with the lemon wedges.

3. To grill, brush the crabs with a little olive oil and sprinkle with salt. Grill, turning once or twice, until browned and firm, 5 to 10 minutes. Brush with more olive oil and serve with lemon or, if you like, melted unsalted butter.

grilled white-and-sweet potato salad

This sharp potato salad is distinguished by its potato combination, its mustard dressing, and its vinegar. If you can't grill the potatoes, brush the slices with olive oil and roast them on a nonstick sheet pan in a hot oven for about 20 minutes, or until browned and tender; turn them once or twice as they cook.

MAKES 8 SERVINGS

TIME: ABOUT 40 MINUTES

2 large, waxy new potatoes, about 1 pound

2 large sweet potatoes, 1 pound total

4 tablespoons extra virgin olive oil

Salt and freshly ground black pepper

1 tablespoon grainy mustard

1 tablespoon sherry or other vinegar, or to taste

1 bunch scallions, both white and green parts, chopped

1. Peel the potatoes and cut them into $1/2$-inch-thick slices, toss them with half the olive oil, and sprinkle them with salt and pepper. In the course of grilling any of the other dishes here, grill the potatoes over direct but not-too-hot heat, turning them as they brown (it doesn't matter much whether the grill is covered, though the potatoes will cook faster if it is).

2. Remove the potato slices as they become tender (they will cook fairly quickly, in 10 to 15 minutes). When they're all done, and fairly cool, toss them with all the remaining ingredients. Taste and adjust the seasoning and serve or cover and refrigerate; bring back to room temperature before serving.

citrus with honey and mint

This dessert—the kind of thing that Jell-O is supposed to imitate—is unusual these days, but it's easy and delicious, a nice use of fruit that's available year-round.

MAKES 8 SERVINGS

TIME: 1½ HOURS, LARGELY UNATTENDED

2 grapefruit

4 medium (or 2 large) navel oranges

4 tangerines

4 temple or other juice oranges

2 tablespoons honey, or to taste

2 tablespoons chopped fresh mint, plus a few mint leaves

2 envelopes unflavored gelatin

1. Over a bowl, cut the grapefruit in half and section as you would to serve it at the table, making sure to catch all the juice; you want small pieces with little or no membrane or pith. Peel the navel oranges and tangerines, then, over the same bowl, trim off most of the white pith that clings to their surface. Separate into sections and cut into small pieces if necessary, again, making sure to catch all the juice. Strain the fruit. Juice the juice oranges and add this to the reserved juice.

2. Toss the fruit with the honey and mint and put them into eight small bowls. Put the juice in a small saucepan and sprinkle the gelatin over the surface. Wait a couple of minutes, then warm the mixture over low heat, stirring to dissolve the gelatin. Cool slightly, then pour the juice mixture over the fruit in the bowls.

3. Refrigerate for about an hour, or until the juice mixture gels. Serve, garnished with additional mint.

a picnic from the mediterranean

HERBED FARMER, GOAT, OR CREAM CHEESE

CHICKEN SALAD TARATOR

COOL COOKED GREENS WITH LEMON

FLATBREADS

OLIVE OIL SUGAR COOKIES

It's not easy to be imaginative or inventive with portable meals, and that's why so many of them are the same. Here's one with a few twists: an herby homemade cheese spread, a wildly different chicken salad, deliciously juicy cold cooked greens, and sweet, crunchy cookies made with olive oil.

KEYS TO SUCCESS

- Fresh thyme will make a huge difference in the cheese. If you only have dried thyme, consider using whatever fresh herb you can lay your hands on, like sage or parsley. Add it to taste.

- The easiest way to cook greens like collards is to boil them in abundant water. When they're done, drain them and plunge them into cold (even ice) water to stop the cooking. Then chop, if you like.

- Some other dishes that could make contributions to this picnic: Mussel and Potato Salad (page 87); Grilled Eggplant Dip (page 124); Roast Tomato Frittata (page 144).

WINE

White, cool, and simple: a Graves would be ideal, but there
are many other choices: Pinot Blanc, Pinot Gris, Pinot Grigio, or a
blend from the south of France.

THE TIMETABLE

- All of this can be made in advance, of course, since you'll be bringing it with you. (The only final preparation is to dress the greens.) The cookies can be prepared a day or two ahead of time, as can the cheese, which should be kept refrigerated. The greens can be cooked and chopped up to 24 hours before eating; the chicken salad is best made the morning of the picnic.

herbed farmer, goat, or cream cheese

A wonderful showcase for any herb, but the thyme-garlic combo is most familiar and probably the most broadly appealing.

MAKES 8 SERVINGS

TIME: 10 MINUTES, PLUS ABOUT 30 MINUTES TO REST

1 pound cold farmer cheese, fresh goat cheese, or cream cheese

1/2 cup sour cream

1 tablespoon fresh thyme leaves, or more to taste

1/2 garlic clove, or more if you like

Salt and freshly ground black pepper

1. Combine all the ingredients in a food processor and blend until smooth. (Alternatively, mince the garlic and mash all the ingredients with a potato masher or fork until fairly smooth, then beat for a few moments with a wire whisk.) Taste and adjust the seasoning as necessary.

2. Scrape into a bowl and refrigerate until stiffened. Serve with crackers, lightly toasted pita, and/or raw vegetable sticks.

chicken salad tarator

The sauce used as a basis for this salad—called skordalia *in Greece and* tara-tor *in Turkey—can be used to top grilled or sautéed meats or chicken, and is a fine substitute for mayonnaise.*

MAKES 4 SERVINGS

TIME: 30 MINUTES

4 ounces good bread

2 cups milk or stock

8 ounces walnuts, about 1 cup

1 large garlic clove

Salt

$1/2$ cup walnut, hazelnut, or olive oil

Freshly ground black pepper

Chili powder or paprika to taste

4 cups shredded or chopped cooked boneless chicken meat

3 cups chopped fresh parsley leaves, washed and dried

1. Soak the bread in the milk or stock. Put the walnuts, garlic, and some salt in the container of a food processor and pulse the machine on and off to grind coarsely. Gently squeeze some of the liquid from the bread and add to the container along with the oil; process until combined but not pureed; add as much of the remaining milk or stock as you need to give the mixture a mayonnaise-like consistency; add the pepper and chili powder or paprika.

2. By hand, fold the sauce together with the chicken and parsley, then taste and adjust the seasoning as necessary.

cool cooked greens with lemon

A classic preparation, useful year-round, and especially convenient when you want to cook the greens in advance.

MAKES 8 SERVINGS

TIME: 20 MINUTES

2 to 3 pounds dark leafy greens, such as collards, kale, or spinach

Several tablespoons extra virgin olive oil

Salt and freshly ground black pepper

4 lemons, cut in half

1. Bring a large pot of water to a boil and salt it. Trim the greens of any stems thicker than $1/4$ inch; discard them. Wash the greens well.

2. Simmer the greens until tender, just a minute or two for spinach, up to 10 minutes or even longer for older, tougher greens. Drain them well and cool them quickly by running them under cold water.

3. Squeeze the greens dry and chop them. (You may prepare the salad in advance to this point; cover and refrigerate for up to a day, then bring to room temperature before proceeding.) Sprinkle with the olive oil, salt, and pepper, and serve with lemon halves.

olive oil sugar cookies

Use light, pure, or extra virgin olive oil for the cookies; the last will give the most distinctive flavor. For a more exotic olive oil cookie, see page 44.

MAKES ABOUT 4 DOZEN

TIME: 30 MINUTES

2$\frac{1}{2}$ cups all-purpose flour

$\frac{1}{2}$ teaspoon baking powder

Pinch of salt

1 cup sugar

2 eggs

$\frac{1}{2}$ cup olive oil

$\frac{3}{4}$ cup milk, or a little more

1 teaspoon vanilla extract

1. Preheat the oven to 375°F. Combine the dry ingredients. Beat the eggs with the olive oil and milk. Use a rubber spatula to stir the liquid mix into the dry one, just until well combined, then stir in the vanilla; if the mixture is stiff, add a little more milk.

2. Drop by rounded teaspoons onto a lightly oiled cookie sheet and bake 12 to 15 minutes, or until lightly browned. Cool a couple of minutes, then remove the cookies from the pan to cool on a rack. Store in a covered tin for up to 3 days.

a grilled meal for everyone

HERBED GREEN SALAD WITH NUT VINAIGRETTE (PAGE 61)

CUMIN-RUBBED LAMB CHOPS WITH CUCUMBER SALAD

GRILLED RED PEPPERS WITH OLIVE OIL AND SHERRY VINEGAR

GRILLED FLATBREADS (PAGE 95)

GRILLED FRUIT SKEWERS WITH GINGER SYRUP

This is a grilled meal that will please just about everyone,
omnivores and vegetarians alike. While it's inarguable that meat
is the centerpiece, the vegetable components are plentiful
and super, and the unusual, delicious grilled dessert
will wow your guests.

KEYS TO SUCCESS

- I like shoulder lamb chops, and not just because they're cheap—their higher percentage of fat makes them juicier, and far more tolerant of overcooking, than their more expensive cousins.

- If you have the time, toast whole cumin (seeds) in a dry skillet for a minute or two, until they become fragrant. Then grind the seeds to a powder in a coffee or spice mill before using it on the lamb.

- Red peppers are the standard for grilling, but if yellow and orange peppers are in the market and not outrageously expensive, mix all three—you can even throw in a green pepper or two.

- Vary the fruit as you like—you can grill almost any fruit as long as it is not so ripe it will fall apart—but be sure to include some bananas, which are really spectacular when treated this way.

WINE

Almost any red will complement this meal, even a fine Bordeaux.
But the rough, inexpensive types will also be appropriate—anything from Zinfandel to chilled Beaujolais.

THE TIMETABLE

- You can make the ginger syrup well in advance, even a day or two.

- An hour or two before you want to eat, start the grill and cook the peppers; if you're grilling a dozen or so, which you should for a large party, they will take up the entire grill.

- Make the cucumber salad, then grill the lamb chops.

- Grill the fruit just before serving it.

cumin-rubbed lamb chops with cucumber salad

Lamb chops are among the best meats to grill. Although they tend to catch fire, they cook so quickly—3 minutes per side is usually more than enough—that there is no time for them to char, and the fire makes the exterior even crisper than it might be otherwise. The cucumbers are best if they're salted, which removes some of their bitterness and makes them extra-crunchy.

MAKES 8 SERVINGS

TIME: 1 HOUR, LARGELY UNATTENDED

About 3 pounds cucumbers, peeled and thinly sliced

Salt

1 cup coarsely chopped fresh mint leaves

4 lemons

8 shoulder or leg lamb chops, or 24 rib or loin chops, about 2 pounds

Freshly ground black pepper to taste

2 tablespoons ground cumin, preferably freshly ground (see Keys to Success)

1. Place the cucumber slices in a colander and sprinkle with salt, just a little more than if you were planning to eat them right away. After 15 to 30 minutes, start a charcoal or wood fire or preheat a gas grill or the broiler; the rack should be about 4 inches from the heat source.

2. When the fire is hot, press the cucumbers to extract as much liquid as possible and toss them with the mint and the juice of one of the lemons. Rub the lamb chops with salt, pepper, and cumin and grill about 3 minutes per side for rare, turning once.

3. Serve each of the lamb chops on a bed of the cucumber salad. Quarter the remaining lemons and serve them to squeeze over the lamb.

grilled red peppers
with olive oil and sherry vinegar

The standard grilled pepper should be a part of every home cook's repertoire.

MAKES 8 SERVINGS

TIME: 30 MINUTES

8 red peppers, washed

4 tablespoons extra virgin olive oil

2 tablespoons sherry vinegar

2 tablespoons capers, drained, optional

Freshly ground black pepper

Salt, optional

1. Start a charcoal or wood fire or preheat a gas grill or the broiler; the rack should be about 4 inches from the heat source. When the fire is hot, put the peppers directly over the heat. Grill, turning as each side blackens, until they collapse, about 15 minutes. Wrap them in foil and cool until you can handle them, then remove the skin, seeds, and stems. You will inevitably shred them in this process, and that's fine.

2. Drizzle the peppers with the olive oil and vinegar, then sprinkle with the capers and some pepper. Taste and add salt, if necessary, then serve.

grilled fruit skewers with ginger syrup

I make these skewers, the creation of my friend Johnny Earles, several times each summer. The bananas, especially, drive everyone wild.

MAKES 8 SERVINGS

TIME: 30 MINUTES

1 cup sugar

$^1/_2$ cup thinly sliced fresh ginger (don't bother to peel it)

4 large or 6 medium bananas, not overly ripe

1 pineapple

4 large peaches

1. Start a gas or charcoal fire; the fire should be quite hot, and the rack positioned 4 to 6 inches from the heat source. Combine the first two ingredients with 1 cup of water in a saucepan over medium heat. Bring to a boil and simmer for 3 minutes. Remove from the heat and let sit while you prepare the fruit.

2. Do not peel the bananas; cut them into 2-inch-long chunks and make a shallow vertical slit in the skin to facilitate peeling at the table. Peel and core the pineapple, then cut it into 2-inch chunks. Pit the peaches and cut them into large chunks.

3. Skewer the fruit. Strain the syrup and brush the fruit lightly with it. Grill the fruit until the pineapple is nicely browned, 2 to 4 minutes per side. As it is grilling, brush occasionally with the syrup.

4. When the fruit is done, brush once more with syrup; serve hot or warm.

a caribbean dinner

CURRIED SWEET POTATO SOUP WITH APRICOT

CRISPY PORK BITS WITH JERK SEASONINGS

COCONUT RICE AND BEANS

FLAN

The Spanish–African–East Indian amalgam that is
Caribbean food is always appropriate in hot weather, and makes
for an unusual dinner. These are among my favorites,
and they combine beautifully.

KEYS TO SUCCESS

- The soup can be served hot or cold; by all means chill it in warm weather, but remember it in winter.

- Pork shoulder is sometimes called Boston butt or picnic. You want it fresh, that is, uncured (not made into ham). It will be very inexpensive.

- To save time, you can make custard instead of "flan"—skip the first step of making the caramel.

- Chile-Fried Shrimp with Scallions and Orange (page 172) would be a good addition to this meal.

WINE

Beer is most appropriate, but a chilled Pinot Noir
or Beaujolais would be terrific.

THE TIMETABLE

- Whether you're reheating it or serving it cold, make the soup as far in advance as you like, up to a couple of days.

- Similarly, you can prepare the pork through the end of Step 2 as much as a day in advance.

- The flan, too, can be made a day early.

- About an hour before you're ready to eat, start the rice and beans. Serve the soup, then grill or sear the meat. Serve the meat with the rice and beans, followed by dessert.

curried sweet potato soup with apricot

Make this soup even richer and sweeter by using half chicken stock and half canned coconut milk.

MAKES 8 SERVINGS

TIME: ABOUT 1 HOUR

2 tablespoons unsalted butter

1 tablespoon curry powder, or to taste

2 large sweet potatoes, about 2 pounds, peeled and cut into chunks

2 cups dried apricots, about 1 pound

Salt

8 cups chicken or other stock

1. Put the butter in a casserole or Dutch oven and turn the heat to medium-high; when the butter melts, add the curry and cook, stirring, for about 30 seconds. Add the sweet potatoes and the apricots and cook, stirring occasionally, until well mixed, a minute or so.

2. Season with salt and add the stock. Turn the heat to high and bring to a boil. Cover and adjust the heat so that the mixture simmers. Cook until the potatoes are very tender, 20 to 30 minutes. If time allows, cool.

3. Place the mixture, in batches if necessary, in the container of a blender and puree until smooth, adding a little water or stock if necessary if the mixture is too thick. (The recipe can be prepared a day or two in advance up to this point; cool, place in a covered container, and refrigerate.) Reheat, adjust the seasoning, and serve.

crispy pork bits
with jerk seasonings

You'll find strongly seasoned, crunchy pork everywhere in Latin America, and it's always irresistible.

MAKES 8 SERVINGS

TIME: 2 HOURS, LARGELY UNATTENDED

3 pounds boneless pork shoulder, trimmed of excess fat and cut into large chunks

10 garlic cloves, crushed

2 tablespoons coriander seeds

1 dried chipotle or other chile

1 cinnamon stick

Several gratings of nutmeg

Salt

1 cup chopped cilantro

4 limes, cut into wedges

1. Put the pork in a deep skillet or wide saucepan; wrap the garlic, coriander, chile, and cinnamon in a piece of cheesecloth and add to the pan, along with the nutmeg and salt. Add water to cover and bring to a boil over high heat. Turn the heat to low and simmer until the pork is very tender, about 1 1/4 hours, adding water as necessary.

2. When the pork is soft, remove the cheesecloth sack and discard it. Raise the heat to medium-high and boil off all the liquid.

3. If you choose not to grill, you can now brown the pork in its own remaining fat. Or, thread the pork onto eight skewers and, when you're ready to eat, grill them lightly on all sides to brown. Garnish with the cilantro and serve with the lime wedges.

coconut rice
and beans

Another classic dish, one that, once you master it, will become routine. I never get tired of it.

MAKES 8 SERVINGS

TIME: 30 MINUTES

3 cans coconut milk, 5 to 6 cups

$2^{1}/_{2}$ cups rice, preferably jasmine

Salt

$1^{1}/_{2}$ cups moist, cooked (or canned) kidney, pinto, pink, or black beans

1. Combine the coconut milk and rice in a saucepan and bring to a boil over medium heat, stirring occasionally. Add some salt, reduce the heat to low, and cover. Cook for 10 minutes, stirring occasionally to make sure the bottom doesn't stick or burn.

2. Uncover and continue to cook, stirring, over low heat until the rice is tender and the mixture is creamy. If the liquid evaporates before the rice is done, stir in some water, about $^{1}/_{2}$ cup at a time, and cook until done. Stir in the beans just about 5 minutes before the rice is finished.

flan

If you use vanilla in place of the cinnamon and nutmeg and omit the caramel (Step 1), call these pots de crème. No matter how you make them, though, be careful not to overcook or the eggs will curdle instead of becoming silky and creamy.

MAKES 8 SERVINGS

TIME: ABOUT 60 MINUTES

1^3/4 cups sugar

3 cups heavy cream, light cream, milk, or a mixture

1/2 teaspoon ground cinnamon

1/2 teaspoon freshly grated nutmeg

3 eggs, plus 3 yolks

Pinch of salt

1. Place 1 cup sugar and 1/4 cup water in a small saucepan. Turn the heat to medium-low and cook, stirring only infrequently, until the sugar liquefies, turns clear, then golden brown, about 15 minutes. Remove from the heat and immediately pour the caramel into the bottom of a large bowl or eight custard cups.

2. Place the cream in a small saucepan with the cinnamon and half the nutmeg and turn the heat to medium. Cook just until it begins to steam.

3. Use a whisk or electric mixer to beat the eggs and yolks with the salt and remaining sugar until pale yellow and fairly thick. Preheat the oven to 300°F and set a kettle of water to boil. Add the cream gradually to the egg mixture, stirring constantly. Pour the mixture into the bowl or custard cups and top with the remaining nutmeg. Place the bowl or cups in a baking pan and pour the hot water in, to within about 1 inch of the top of the bowl or cups. Bake until the mixture is not quite set—it should wobble just a little in the middle—about 30 minutes for the cups, longer if you're baking in a bowl. Use your judgment; cream sets up faster than milk. Serve warm, at room temperature, or cold, within a day.

a modern barbecue

GRILLED EGGPLANT DIP

GRILLED FLATBREADS (PAGE 95)

SLOW-GRILLED CHICKEN WITH CHIPOTLE-PEACH SALSA

SLOW-GRILLED RIBS

GRILLED WHITE-AND-SWEET POTATO SALAD (PAGE 102)

RASPBERRY FOOL

"Modern," because it integrates the best grilling techniques with simple (in some cases no) sauces, no marinating, and no burning. The all-grilled meal ends with a simple, easily made dessert that can be produced only in midsummer.

KEYS TO SUCCESS

- Buy the firmest eggplant you can find; smaller is usually better, because it is likely to have fewer seeds.

- Ribs are easiest to grill if you buy them in racks; one rack will usually feed at least two people, though if you're making the chicken as well, you can definitely make less, just two racks for eight people.

WINE

Cold rosé would be my first choice, or something red and rough, or a light wine like Beaujolais, lightly chilled.

THE TIMETABLE

The advantage of this menu is that so much of it can be prepared in advance; you can spend the day grilling, but slowly and without much effort, and then, when your guests arrive, finish up without breaking a sweat.

- Several hours before eating, fire up the grill and do the eggplant and potatoes, then turn down the heat (or let it cool down) and cook the ribs, allowing plenty of time.

- When you're ready to eat, quickly grill the flatbreads and serve them with the eggplant dip. Grill the chicken, then reheat the racks of ribs; serve them separately or together, with the potato salad.

- Make the fool no more than an hour before serving.

grilled eggplant dip

Grilling is an important part of this dish, as it gives the eggplant a smoky flavor that's hard to come by otherwise.

MAKES 8 SERVINGS

TIME: ABOUT 1 HOUR

2 medium or 4 small eggplant, about 1 pound total

$^1/_4$ cup fresh lemon juice

$^1/_4$ cup extra virgin olive oil

$^1/_2$ teaspoon minced garlic, or to taste

Salt and freshly ground black pepper

Minced fresh parsley leaves

1. Start a charcoal, wood, or gas grill; pierce the eggplant in several places with a thin-bladed knife or skewer. Grill, turning occasionally, until the eggplant collapses and the skin blackens, 15 to 30 minutes depending on size. Remove and cool.

2. When the eggplant is cool enough to handle, part the skin (if it hasn't split on its own), scoop out the flesh, and mince it finely. Mix it with the lemon juice, oil, garlic, salt, and pepper. Taste and adjust the seasonings, then garnish with the parsley and serve with the Grilled Flatbreads.

slow-grilled chicken with chipotle-peach salsa

This is the best way to grill chicken without burning it; you can serve it hot or at room temperature.

MAKES 8 SERVINGS

TIME: 45 TO 60 MINUTES

2 chickens, cut into 8 or 10 pieces each

Salt and freshly ground black pepper

Chipotle-Peach Salsa (recipe follows)

1. Start a charcoal, wood, or gas fire on a covered grill big enough to bank the coals to one side once they get hot (on a gas grill, turn the heat to high on one side and keep it off on the other). When the grill is hot, put the chicken on the less hot part of the grill, skin up, and cover the grill. Walk away for about 20 minutes.

2. When the bottom of the chicken is lightly browned and the meat is beginning to look cooked, turn the meat over, still on the cool side of the grill. Cover again and check after about 10 minutes. When the skin is lightly browned, turn again. Continue to cook on the cool side of the grill until the chicken looks close to done, another 10 to 20 minutes.

3. At this point, uncover and move the chicken to the hot side of the grill or, if you have a gas grill, simply ignite the portion of the grill under the chicken. Now cook attentively, turning the chicken as it cooks until it is brown and crisp all over, 5 to 10 minutes more. Serve hot, warm, or at room temperature, sprinkled with salt and lots of pepper, and with Chipotle-Peach Salsa.

chipotle-peach salsa

MAKES ABOUT 4 CUPS

TIME: 15 MINUTES, PLUS TIME TO REST

4 cups pitted, diced peaches, cut into $^1/_4$-inch dice

1 cup diced red bell pepper, stemmed, seeded, and cut into $^1/_4$-inch dice

2 chiles in adobo, pureed

$^1/_4$ cup fresh lime juice

$^1/_2$ cup minced cilantro

2 tablespoons sugar

Chiles in adobo are chipotles (wood-smoked jalapeños) in a kind of tomato sauce, sold in cans. They're available at any market with a good selection of Mexican foods. If you can't find one, substitute a hot chili powder or even cayenne.

Use a pineapple or nectarines instead of peaches, if you prefer.

Combine all the ingredients and let them "marry" for up to 1 hour before serving.

slow-grilled ribs

This is the way to get tender, moist ribs without burning them. They take some time, but not much attention.

MAKES 8 SERVINGS

TIME: AT LEAST 2 HOURS

2 to 4 racks of ribs (see Keys to Success)

Salt and freshly ground black pepper

1. Start a not-too-fierce charcoal, wood, or gas fire on a covered grill big enough to bank the coals to one side once they get hot (on a gas grill, turn the heat to medium on one side and keep it off on the other; if there are three burners, you can light the two side ones and cook in the middle). When the grill is hot, put the ribs on the less hot part of the grill and cover the grill. Walk away for about 30 minutes.

2. Turn the ribs and continue to cook them, adding to the fire if necessary. They should be very slowly browning, firming up, and drying out. When the meat begins to pull away from the bone and the meat between the bones is easily pierced with a thin-bladed knife, the meat is nearly done. At this point you can cool the ribs slightly, then wrap well in foil and put in the refrigerator, or continue to cook.

3. When you're ready to serve the ribs, brown them on both sides over direct heat, being careful not to burn; this will take only 10 minutes or so. When they're done, season them with salt and pepper and serve.

raspberry fool

A classic English dessert that dates back to the sixteenth century, at least.

MAKES 8 SERVINGS

TIME: 20 MINUTES

4 cups raspberries

1 cup plus 1 tablespoon superfine or confectioners' sugar, plus more if needed

1 cup heavy cream, preferably not ultrapasteurized

1. Toss about two-thirds of the berries with $^1/_2$ cup of the sugar; set aside. Puree the remaining berries in a blender with $^1/_2$ cup sugar. Force the puree through a sieve to remove the seeds. Taste; the puree should be quite sweet. If it is not, add a little more sugar.

2. Beat the cream with 1 tablespoon sugar, until it holds soft peaks. Stir in the puree, then fold in the sugared berries. Taste and add more sugar if necessary. Serve immediately or refrigerate for up to an hour, no longer.

autumn

a simple but grand meal

PROSCIUTTO, FIG, AND PARMESAN ROLLS

ROAST SHRIMP WITH TOMATO, ZUCCHINI, AND ONION

SLOW-COOKED DUCK LEGS WITH OLIVES

BREAD

RAW BEET SALAD (PAGE 4)

CHOCOLATE MOUSSE (PAGE 14)

These are the kinds of dishes that welcome you back to the kitchen after a hot summer, dishes that warm the kitchen while their aromas fill the house. The cooking is relaxing and the results will be enormously popular.

KEYS TO SUCCESS

- Make sure, please, to use prosciutto from Italy; it makes a huge difference.

- You may need to preorder duck legs; take this into account so you don't get stuck.

- If you want to expand on this meal, add another simple starter, like Fennel with Olive Oil Dipping Sauce (page 86) or Skewered Crisp Shiitakes with Garlic (page 197).

WINE

Red, for sure, preferably something rich and wonderful.
A classified Bordeaux or cru bourgeois would not be out of place;
good California Cabernet would also be wonderful.

THE TIMETABLE

- Make the mousse and, about 2 hours before you want to eat, begin cooking the duck legs. Attend to them as necessary, which will be intermittently.

- Prepare the prosciutto rolls any time within that same 2-hour window; let them sit at room temperature; add the oil just before serving.

- In the remaining hour, make the beet salad and, finally, while people are munching on the prosciutto rolls, the shrimp. When that's eaten, finish the duck and serve it with the beet salad.

prosciutto, fig, and parmesan rolls

A simple, stand-up, make-in-advance starter.

MAKES ABOUT 20 ROLLS, ENOUGH FOR
8 PEOPLE

TIME: 20 MINUTES

$^1/_2$ pound prosciutto, sliced very thin

About $^1/_4$ pound Parmesan, sliced wafer-thin

8 to 10 dried figs, stemmed and cut into about 3 strips each

Truffle or olive oil

1. Cut each piece of prosciutto in half the long way; on each piece, put a slice of Parmesan and a strip of fig. Roll up the long way, pressing so that the meat sticks to itself. Cover with plastic wrap if not serving right away.

2. Serve within 2 hours, drizzling with truffle oil just before serving.

roast shrimp with tomato, zucchini, and onion

This is a dish I first ate in Istanbul, a bubbly casserole of shrimp, tomatoes, and vegetables, in which the dominant seasonings are basil and butter (though you can use olive oil if you prefer). It's great over pasta; this amount will easily "sauce" a couple of pounds of linguine.

MAKES 8 SERVINGS

TIME: 45 MINUTES

12 plum tomatoes, about 2 pounds

2 large onions

4 medium zucchini, about 1 pound

Salt

$1/4$ teaspoon cayenne, or to taste

8 tablespoons unsalted butter (1 stick) or olive oil

3 pounds peeled shrimp

1 cup roughly chopped fresh basil

1. Preheat the oven to 500°F. Chop the tomatoes, onions, and zucchini into roughly $1/2$-inch cubes; combine them in a large, broad ovenproof skillet or casserole. Add the salt, cayenne, and half the butter; place in the oven. Roast 10 to 15 minutes, shaking the pan once or twice.

2. Remove the pan from the oven and stir well; at some point, the tomatoes will break up and become "saucy." (If this does not happen, roast another 5 minutes. If it still does not happen, you have exceptionally dry plum tomatoes; continue with the recipe.) Add the shrimp.

3. Roast 5 minutes, then stir and add the remaining butter. Roast until the shrimp are pink and firm, about 5 minutes more. Taste and adjust the seasoning, stir in the basil, and serve.

slow-cooked duck legs with olives

Unless you've made your own duck confit, you may never have cooked duck legs by themselves; but in many ways they're superior to both duck breasts and whole birds. They're quite lean, and just a quick trimming of the excess fat is all that's necessary. Given proper cooking—that is, long, slow cooking—they become fork-tender and richly flavorful, reminiscent of some of the "lesser" cuts of beef and pork, like brisket and cheek. Finally, it's easy enough to cook enough legs for eight—which is hardly the case with whole duck!

MAKES 8 SERVINGS

TIME: 2 HOURS, LARGELY UNATTENDED

8 duck legs

10 or more garlic cloves

2 cups olives, preferably a combination of green and black

Several thyme sprigs

One 28-ounce can tomatoes, with their juice

1 large onion, roughly chopped, optional

2 carrots, roughly chopped, optional

2 celery stalks, roughly chopped, optional

Salt and freshly ground black pepper

Chopped fresh parsley

1. Trim all visible fat from the duck legs, then lay them in a large, broad skillet; they can overlap if necessary. Turn the heat to medium and add the garlic, olives, thyme, and tomatoes. Add the onion, carrots, and celery, if you are using. Season with salt and pepper. When the mixture reaches a lively simmer, turn the heat to low and cover.

2. Cook, checking occasionally—the mixture should be gently bubbling when you remove the cover—until the duck is very tender, about 1 1/2 hours. Remove the duck to a warm plate and cover (or place in a very low oven), then turn the heat to medium-high under the remaining sauce. Cook, stirring occasionally, until the mixture is reduced to a thick, saucelike consistency, about 10 minutes. Spoon over the duck legs, garnish with the chopped parsley, and serve.

a mostly fish dinner for fall

CLAM STEW WITH POTATOES AND PARSLEY PUREE

ROAST STRIPED BASS WITH TOMATOES AND OLIVES

GOLDEN PILAF

APPLE CRISP

This is an eclectic menu, with themes from all over
the Mediterranean as well as the United States. But the dishes
complement one another nicely, and they're all delicious.

KEYS TO SUCCESS

- Hard-shell clams, often called littlenecks, cherrystones, or quahogs, are a must for this chowder; cockles, which are related but smaller, will also work well. Steamers (which have softer shells) will make the chowder sandy.

- In place of striped bass, often available only in the Northeast and even there just seasonally, you can use red snapper, sea bass, or rockfish.

- Big Chopped Salad with Vinaigrette (page 148) will fill out this menu well, as will Steamed Broccoli with Beurre Noisette (page 249). And if you like, substitute Salmon and Tomatoes Cooked in Foil (page 49) for the striped bass dish.

WINE

You can go with a fruity red here, if you like—Pinot Noir, Zinfandel, or something similar—but a crisp, not too rich Chardonnay, especially from Chablis, is probably best.

THE TIMETABLE

- Make the crisp first; even if you want to eat it hot or warm, you can put it in the oven for a few minutes just before serving.

- You can wash the clams hours or even a day in advance; keep them in a large bowl or colander set over a bowl, uncovered, in the refrigerator.

- When it comes time to cook, start the pilaf, make the tomato sauce, and get the fish ready to cook. Prepare and serve the clam stew, keeping the pilaf warm if it finishes early, and holding off on roasting the fish.

- When your guests are done with the chowder, roast the fish and serve it with the pilaf.

clam stew with potatoes and parsley puree

This is essentially a clam chowder but one that, although it is no more elaborate than any of the others, is less soupy, more colorful, and supremely "clammy." The departures from American tradition include a strong whiff of garlic and a bright green puree of parsley.

MAKES 8 SERVINGS

TIME: 40 MINUTES

8 pounds small clams (see Keys to Success)

24 ounces waxy potatoes, peeled and cut into $^1/_4$-inch dice

$1^1/_2$ cups dry white wine

2 bunches parsley, thick stems removed and tied in a bundle

2 garlic cloves

$^1/_2$ cup extra virgin olive oil

Salt

1. Wash the clams well, in several changes of water, until the water contains no traces of sand. Put in a wide, deep skillet or saucepan along with the potatoes, wine, and thick parsley stems. Cover and turn the heat to high.

2. While the clams and potatoes are cooking, combine the parsley leaves and thin stems in a blender with the garlic and oil. Puree, adding water as necessary (it will be $^1/_2$ cup or more) to make a smooth puree. Add salt to taste and transfer to a bowl.

3. Cook the clam-potato mixture until the potatoes are tender, about 15 minutes. Remove the bundle of thick stems and discard, then stir about half the puree into the mixture and serve, passing the rest at the table. (Any clams that do not open can be pried open at the table with a butter knife.)

roast striped bass with tomatoes and olives

Striped bass, one of our most firm-fleshed and delicious fish, is plentiful in the fall. Unlike many white-fleshed fish, it must be cooked through in order to become tender. To make this dish even better, use roasted tomatoes from the frittata on page 144.

MAKES 8 SERVINGS

TIME: 20 MINUTES

12 plum tomatoes, cut in half

$^1/_4$ cup extra virgin olive oil

About 50 good, large black olives, such as kalamata

3 to 4 pounds striped bass fillet, skin on or off

Salt and freshly ground black pepper

Fresh thyme leaves, optional

1. Preheat the oven to 500°F. Combine the tomatoes and half the olive oil in a small saucepan with 1 tablespoon of water and the olives and cook over medium heat, stirring occasionally, until the mixture is saucy; keep warm.

2. Rub the fish all over with the remaining olive oil, then sprinkle with the salt and pepper. Place on a baking sheet or roasting pan, preferably nonstick, and put in the oven.

3. Roast the fish until a thin-bladed knife penetrates it with little resistance, about 10 minutes. When it is done, spoon the sauce over it, cut into 8 pieces, garnish, if desired, and serve.

golden pilaf

The classic rice dish from the eastern Mediterranean, easier than risotto but no less delicious, is largely dependent on the quality of the rice and the stock. Use basmati rice for the best texture, and a pilaf that is so perfect it can actually be reheated successfully.

MAKES 8 SERVINGS

TIME: 60 MINUTES, LARGELY UNATTENDED

3 cups chicken, beef, or vegetable stock

1 teaspoon saffron threads

$^{1}/_{4}$ cup ($^{1}/_{2}$ stick) unsalted butter or extra virgin olive oil

1 large onion, chopped

Salt

2 cups long-grain white rice

Freshly ground black pepper

1 cup chopped fresh parsley

$^{1}/_{4}$ cup fresh lemon juice

1. Gently warm the stock with the saffron in a small saucepan while you proceed with the recipe. Put the butter in a large, deep skillet that can later be covered and turn the heat to medium. Add the onion and a large pinch of salt and cook, stirring occasionally, until the onion turns translucent, 5 to 10 minutes. Add the rice and cook, stirring occasionally, until the rice is glossy and begins to brown, 3 to 5 minutes. Season with salt and pepper.

2. Add the warm stock and stir. Raise the heat and bring the mixture to a boil; cook for a minute or two, then reduce the heat to low and cover. Cook about 15 minutes, or until most of the liquid is absorbed. Turn the heat to the absolute minimum (if you have an electric stove, turn the heat off and let the pan sit on the burner) and let rest another 15 to 30 minutes. Stir in the parsley and lemon juice and serve.

apple crisp

In place of apples, you can use pears here, or a mixture. In fact, this is a universal crisp recipe, and will work with just about any fruit. Almost needless to say, it's great with vanilla ice cream.

MAKES 8 SERVINGS

TIME: ABOUT 1 HOUR

6 cups peeled, cored, and sliced apples or other fruit

1 teaspoon ground cinnamon

Juice of $1/2$ lemon

$2/3$ cup brown sugar, or to taste

5 tablespoons cold unsalted butter, cut into bits, plus more for greasing the pan

$1/2$ cup rolled oats

$1/2$ cup all-purpose flour

$1/4$ cup shredded unsweetened coconut, optional

$1/4$ cup chopped nuts, optional

Dash of salt

1. Preheat the oven to 400°F. Toss the fruit with half the cinnamon, the lemon juice, and 1 tablespoon of the sugar, and spread it in a lightly buttered 8-inch square or 9-inch round baking pan.

2. Combine all the other ingredients—including the remaining cinnamon and sugar and the chopped nuts, if you're using—in the container of a food processor and pulse a few times, then process a few seconds more until everything is well incorporated but not uniform. (To mix the ingredients by hand, soften the butter slightly, toss together the dry ingredients, then work in the butter with your fingertips, a pastry blender, or a fork.)

3. Spread the topping over the apples and bake 30 to 40 minutes, until the topping is browned and the apples are tender. Serve hot, warm, or at room temperature.

an informal buffet

ROAST TOMATO FRITTATA

KALE, SAUSAGE, AND MUSHROOM STEW

BREAD

BIG CHOPPED SALAD WITH VINAIGRETTE

PUMPKIN PANNA COTTA

This is far from a fancy spread. Rather it's a buffet you can set out any time, for friends or family, and, if you have a means by which you can keep the stew hot—even a small candle set under it will do the trick—one you can leave out for quite a while.

KEYS TO SUCCESS

- You might as well roast a couple of dozen tomatoes; it will take no more work, and you will find a way to eat them, believe me; they're great in Roast Striped Bass with Tomatoes and Olives (page 139).

- Ordinary, old-fashioned Italian pork sausage is best. The new designer sausages contain so little fat that they are inevitably tough, if not flavorless.

- If you choose to use fresh pumpkin for the panna cotta, steam a few peeled chunks over boiling water until very tender, then puree in a blender. Canned pumpkin (or squash) is perfectly acceptable.

WINE

A hearty but simple red, like an inexpensive
Côtes du Rhone or Châteauneuf-du-Pape.

THE TIMETABLE

- Everything here can be made in advance. Start with the panna cotta, which can sit overnight (though it will be ready within a couple of hours of making it).

- Prepare the salad. Add the dressing just before serving.

- Roast the tomatoes whenever you have a chance, even a couple of days ahead of time.

- The stew can be done at the last minute, or a few hours ahead of time. The frittata is fine served warm, so begin making that about an hour before you want to eat.

roast tomato frittata

Roast tomatoes, the essential ingredient in this frittata, are great by themselves, in salsas and sauces, or as a garnish for grilled or roasted fish or meat. To serve, cut the frittata into cubes or small slices to make for easy handling; it's better eaten with toothpicks or straight from the hand than with a fork and knife.

MAKES 8 SERVINGS

TIME: 30 MINUTES

12 plum tomatoes

$1/4$ cup extra virgin olive oil

4 garlic cloves

Several thyme sprigs

Salt

4 small fingerling potatoes, or 1 medium thin-skinned potato

4 small onions, or 1 large onion

3 tablespoons unsalted butter or extra virgin olive oil

8 eggs

$1/2$ cup freshly grated Parmesan

$1/2$ cup minced fresh parsley leaves

Freshly ground black pepper

1. Preheat the oven to 500°F. Core the tomatoes (cut a small, cone-shaped wedge from their stem ends), cut them in half, and use a paring knife or spoon to scoop out the seeds and pulp. Spread about half the oil on a nonstick baking sheet that will accommodate the tomatoes adequately without crowding, then add the tomatoes. Distribute the garlic and thyme among the tomatoes; drizzle with the remaining oil and some salt. Roast, turning the pan in the oven once for even cooking, for about 30 minutes, or until the tomatoes are shriveled and a little blackened. Remove from the oven and cool while you proceed with the recipe.

2. Lower the oven temperature to 350°F. Wash the potatoes (peeling isn't necessary) and cut them into slices somewhat less than $1/4$ inch thick. Peel the onions; if they're small just cut them in half; if larger, into small wedges.

3. Put the butter in a 10-inch ovenproof skillet, preferably nonstick, and turn the heat to medium-

high. When the butter melts, add the potatoes and onions and cook, stirring only occasionally, until the potatoes are nicely browned on both sides. Meanwhile, lightly beat the eggs in a bowl; stir in the Parmesan and parsley, along with some salt and pepper.

4. When the potatoes are ready, turn the heat to low and wait a minute, then add the eggs. If necessary, move the solids around so they are evenly distributed in the egg mixture. Cook until the frittata is set on the edges, then transfer to the oven and bake until the mixture is barely set on top. Serve in wedges, hot or at room temperature.

kale, sausage, and mushroom stew

By building this stew one ingredient at a time—in a manner not unlike that of making soup—the process is streamlined and nearly everything is browned. This makes the flavors so complex that the stew needs no stock to finish it off. (Should you have some stock on hand, however, by all means use it instead of some of the water.) To make this stew even tastier, use a mixture of mushrooms, or add a few reconstituted dried porcini, and use their strained soaking liquid to replace some of the water.

MAKES 8 SERVINGS

TIME: 30 TO 40 MINUTES

1 tablespoon extra virgin olive oil

1 1/2 to 2 pounds Italian sausage, sweet or hot, cut into 1-inch or smaller pieces

2 pounds kale, leaves stripped from stems (stems reserved)

1 pound mushrooms, trimmed and sliced

2 tablespoons roughly chopped garlic

2 tablespoons hot paprika or crushed red pepper flakes, or to taste

Salt and freshly ground black pepper

4 cups water or stock

1. Put the olive oil in a large, deep skillet or casserole and turn the heat to medium-high; a minute later, add the sausage and cook without stirring until the sausage browns well on one side, about 5 minutes. Meanwhile, chop the stems of the kale into about 1/2-inch lengths and shred the leaves.

2. Stir the sausage and let it brown a bit more. Remove it with a slotted spoon (don't worry if it isn't cooked through). Cook the mushrooms in the remaining fat with the heat still on medium-high, stirring occasionally, until lightly browned, about 10 minutes. Remove with a slotted spoon and keep warm.

3. Add the kale stems and cook, stirring frequently, until they begin to brown, 3 or 4 minutes. Turn the heat to medium and add the garlic, paprika, kale leaves, salt, and pepper; stir and cook for about 1 minute. Return the sausage to the pan and add the water. Raise the heat to high and cook for about 5

minutes, stirring occasionally and scraping the bottom of the pan with a wooden spoon. Add more salt and pepper to taste and ladle into bowls, topping with the reserved mushrooms.

big chopped salad
with vinaigrette

Please, see this ingredients list as a series of suggestions rather than dogma—a chopped salad can contain any combination that appeals to you, including raw vegetables like broccoli or cauliflower, or crunchy cabbages like bok choi, as well as nuts, seeds, and fruit.

MAKES 8 SERVINGS

TIME: 30 MINUTES

1 large head romaine lettuce

1 bunch arugula

1 bunch watercress

2 medium cucumbers, or
1 English cucumber

1 bunch radishes

2 yellow or red bell peppers

2 carrots

2 celery stalks

1 small sweet onion, like Vidalia

$^3/_4$ cup extra virgin olive oil

$^1/_3$ cup, approximately, good vinegar

1 shallot, minced

1 tablespoon Dijon mustard

Salt and freshly ground black pepper

1. Wash and dry all the vegetables as necessary. Roughly chop the greens and place them in a big bowl.

2. Peel the cucumbers, then cut them in half lengthwise; seed if necessary and chop into $^1/_2$-inch dice. Trim the radishes and chop into $^1/_2$-inch dice. Seed and core the peppers and chop into $^1/_2$-inch dice. Peel the carrots and chop into $^1/_2$-inch dice. Chop the celery into $^1/_2$-inch dice. Peel and mince the onion. Toss all the vegetables with the greens.

3. Combine the oil, vinegar, shallot, and mustard and beat with a fork or wire whisk, or emulsify in a blender or with an immersion blender. Season with salt and pepper, then taste and adjust the seasoning as necessary.

4. Just before serving, toss the salad with the dressing.

pumpkin "panna cotta"

Panna cotta is the simplest to make of all legitimate custard desserts, because the gelatin makes it foolproof. If you have never tackled it, you're going to be surprised at how easy it is.

MAKES 8 SERVINGS

TIME: 20 MINUTES, PLUS TIME TO CHILL

$1^1/2$ cups milk

2 envelopes unflavored gelatin

$1^1/2$ cups heavy cream

$1^1/2$ cups pureed pumpkin, squash, or sweet potato

$3/4$ cup sugar

$1/2$ teaspoon ground cinnamon

1. Put $1/2$ cup of the milk in a 6- or 8-cup saucepan and sprinkle the gelatin over it. Let it sit for 5 minutes. Meanwhile, blend together the remaining milk, cream, pumpkin, sugar, and cinnamon. The mixture should be perfectly smooth, so it's best to use a blender.

2. Turn the heat under the saucepan to low and cook the milk, stirring occasionally, until the gelatin dissolves. Pour in the cream mixture and turn the heat to medium. Cook, stirring occasionally, until steam rises. Turn off the heat and ladle or pour into eight 4-ounce ramekins or other containers. Chill until firm (you may unmold them) and serve with crème fraîche or whipped cream if you like.

a cool-weather feast with asian flavors

RICH CHICKEN-NOODLE SOUP WITH GINGER

BROILED BLUEFISH OR MACKEREL WITH GREEN TEA SALT

SPARERIBS, KOREAN-STYLE

HERBED GREEN SALAD WITH SOY VINAIGRETTE (PAGE 38)

COCONUT RICE PUDDING (PAGE 212)

A mix of simply executed Asian-American dishes (none of these is strictly traditional, though all have legitimate roots), which, taken together, makes for a surprisingly elegant meal.

KEYS TO SUCCESS

- The chicken soup is at its best when made with homemade broth, but there is so much added flavor that it will still be delicious if you start with canned.

- The green tea/salt mixture is at its best on dark, full-flavored fish like bluefish and mackerel, but it would be fine on swordfish or even salmon. Green tea is sold in bulk at most stores specializing in Asian foods.

- Have the butcher cut the ribs into 2-inch sections; this will make them easier to cook and to eat.

- This is a large meal, one that would still be adequate if you did without the fish or meat.

WINE

The flavors of Chardonnay and oak marry well with these dishes; look for something from northern California.

THE TIMETABLE

- Start the rice pudding and spareribs first.

- While you're keeping an eye on them, grind the tea, begin the soup, and put together the ingredients for the salad.

- Serve the soup and, while the bowls are being cleared, broil the fish. Serve it separately and, when it's done, follow it with the ribs and salad.

rich chicken-noodle soup with ginger

Buy rice "vermicelli," the thinnest rice noodles sold. Substitute angel hair pasta (you'll have to boil it separately) if you like.

MAKES 8 SERVINGS

TIME: 30 MINUTES

3/4 pound fine rice noodles

12 cups chicken stock

1 dried chile

2 tablespoons finely minced ginger

2 bunches scallions

1 pound boneless chicken breast, skin removed and cut into 1/2-inch cubes

1/2 pound fresh shiitake mushrooms (stems should be reserved for stock or discarded), sliced

1/4 cup nam pla (Thai fish sauce) or soy sauce, or to taste

Salt

1/2 cup roughly chopped cilantro

1. Soak the rice noodles in very hot water to cover. Meanwhile, put the stock in a large saucepan with the chile and ginger and turn the heat to medium. Trim the scallions; chop the white part and add it to the simmering stock. Chop the green part and set aside.

2. After about 15 minutes of simmering, remove the chile. Drain the noodles and add them, along with the chicken breast and mushrooms. Stir and adjust the heat so the mixture continues to simmer. When the chicken is cooked through, about 10 minutes, add the nam pla. Taste and adjust the seasoning—add more nam pla or soy sauce or some salt if necessary, along with the cilantro and reserved scallions—then serve.

broiled bluefish or mackerel with green tea salt

Whether you have a "dedicated" spice grinder, or a coffee grinder that you use occasionally for spices, it should be cleaned thoroughly before processing tea in it. There are two ways to do this (in either case please remember to unplug the appliance before beginning). You can wipe it out well, first with a barely damp paper towel and then with a dry one. Or, grind a couple of tablespoons of rice to a powder, dispose of that, and then wipe with a paper towel.

MAKES 8 SERVINGS

TIME: 15 MINUTES

About 3 pounds bluefish or mackerel fillets

2 tablespoons dark sesame oil

2 tablespoons powdered green tea

1 tablespoon coarse salt

2 limes, quartered

1. Preheat the broiler; you want the heating element as close as possible to the surface of the fish, as little as 2 inches. Arrange the fish in a broiling pan, skin side down, and brush the surface lightly with sesame oil. Mix together the tea and salt.

2. Broil the fish, checking once or twice to make sure it is browning but not burning; lower the rack if necessary. When the fish is browned and a thin-bladed knife penetrates it with little resistance, it is done; total cooking time in a good broiler will be about 5 minutes.

3. Sprinkle the fish liberally with the tea-salt mixture and serve with lime wedges.

spareribs, korean-style

This preparation results in ribs that are dark, glossy, and so tender that just a tug of the teeth will pull them off the bone.

MAKES 8 SERVINGS

TIME: 45 TO 60 MINUTES

6 to 8 pounds spareribs, cut into 2-inch sections

1/2 cup sesame seeds

1/4 cup chopped garlic

1/2 cup sugar

10 nickel-sized pieces of ginger

1 cup soy sauce

1/4 cup sesame oil

Salt and freshly ground black pepper

1 cup chopped scallions

1. Put a large skillet that can hold the ribs in one layer over high heat and add the ribs and 1 cup water. Boil, turning the ribs occasionally, until the liquid has evaporated, then reduce the heat to medium and brown the ribs in their own fat, turning occasionally, for about 5 minutes. Meanwhile, toast the sesame seeds by putting them in a small skillet over medium heat and shaking the pan occasionally until they brown slightly and begin to pop.

2. Add the garlic and half the sesame seeds and stir; cook 30 seconds. Add the sugar, ginger, soy, half the sesame oil, and another 1/2 cup of water; turn the heat to medium-high, and cook, turning occasionally, until the liquid is thick and dark, 10 to 15 minutes. If the ribs are tender at this point, they're ready. If not, add another 1/2 cup of water and continue cooking.

3. Add salt and pepper to taste and the remaining sesame seeds and sesame oil. Stir once, sprinkle with the scallions, and serve.

a holiday goose

CREAM OF SPINACH SOUP

BRAISED GOOSE WITH PEARS OR APPLES

ROASTED NEW POTATOES WITH ROSEMARY

HERBED GREEN SALAD WITH NUT VINAIGRETTE (PAGE 61)

CRANBERRY CLAFOUTI

There is no more celebratory food than goose, but when it is roasted it is difficult to carve and can be disappointing. Braising it, especially with fruit, is a different approach that works brilliantly. Start the meal with creamy spinach soup, complement the goose with roast potatoes and a simple salad, finish with a festive cranberry dessert, and you have a meal fit for Thanksgiving—or any other fall occasion.

KEYS TO SUCCESS

- Note that unlike most of the menus here, this one is designed to serve six. If you want a similar menu to feed eight or more, substitute Coq au Vin with Prunes (page 11) for the goose.

- For super-creamy spinach soup, use cream. For a lighter version, use whole milk (I don't recommend skim or low-fat milk here). You could substitute almost any green vegetable for the spinach, as long as you cook it until it is very tender.

- See if you can get the butcher to cut up the goose for you. If not, treat it like a chicken and take your time; the pieces need not be uniform or especially neat—the dish will look great and be delicious in any case.

- If you don't feel like making potatoes, the goose is also terrific with buttered noodles.

WINE

The best option is a good Pinot Noir (red Burgundy); Cabernet Sauvignon (red Bordeaux) would be a close second.

THE TIMETABLE

- The spinach soup can be made in advance and reheated.

- While the goose is braising, you can prepare the potatoes and the salad (don't dress the salad until the last minute).

- As late in the process as you can (even after dinner is fine), assemble the clafouti. Bake it while you're eating or after you've finished; it's best warm.

cream of spinach soup

Always be careful when pureeing hot soup; if time allows, the safest route is to cool the soup thoroughly before pureeing it. If you're in a hurry, at least cool it to not much more than body temperature (resting the cooking pan in a larger one filled with ice water is the most efficient way to do this) before pureeing. To reduce the chance of spattering, pulse the blender on and off a couple of times before leaving it on, and hold the top down until you're sure it's not going anywhere.

MAKES 6 SERVINGS

TIME: 30 MINUTES

2 pounds spinach, well washed and trimmed of thick stems (or two 10-ounce packages frozen spinach, partially thawed)

2 large white onions, roughly chopped

6 cups chicken or other stock

A grating of nutmeg

Salt and freshly ground black pepper

2 cups heavy or light cream or half-and-half or whole milk (see Keys to Success)

1. Combine the spinach, onions, and stock in a large saucepan and turn the heat to medium-high. Bring to a boil, then lower the heat so the mixture barely bubbles and cook, stirring occasionally, until the spinach is very tender, about 10 minutes. Turn off the heat, add the nutmeg and a sprinkling of salt and pepper, and cool for a few minutes.

2. Working in batches, puree in a blender. Return to the pan, add the cream, and, over medium-low heat, reheat gently, stirring occasionally. When the soup is hot, taste and adjust the seasoning and serve.

braised goose
with pears or apples

Any dried fruit can be used in this preparation, but dried pears and dried apples hold their shape better and are a little less sweet than prunes and apricots; there's no reason you can't substitute, however, or combine.

MAKES 6 SERVINGS

TIME: ABOUT 3 HOURS, LARGELY

UNATTENDED

1 goose, cut into serving pieces, excess fat removed (see Keys to Success)

Salt and freshly ground black pepper

$^{1}/_{2}$ cup diced bacon or pancetta, optional

2 large onions, roughly chopped

4 bay leaves

A few thyme sprigs

$^{1}/_{2}$ pound dried pears or apples

2 cups dry white wine

1 tablespoon dry white wine, Champagne, or sherry vinegar

About 2 pounds pears or apples, peeled, cored, and sliced

1. Turn the heat to medium-high under a casserole or deep skillet, at least 12 inches across; a minute later, add the goose pieces, skin side down. Cook, rearranging the pieces now and then so that they brown evenly, until nicely browned and rendered of fat, 10 to 15 minutes. Sprinkle with salt and pepper and turn; brown 2 or 3 minutes on the meat side. Remove the goose and pour off all but a tablespoon of the fat.

2. If you're using it, cook the bacon in the same skillet, over medium-high heat, until brown and crisp all over, about 10 minutes. Add the onions, bay leaves, and thyme, and cook, stirring occasionally, and seasoning with more salt and pepper, until the onions are softened, about 10 minutes. Add the dried fruit and cook another minute or two, stirring occasionally. Add the wine and raise the heat to high; cook until the wine is reduced by about half, 5 minutes or so.

3. Return the goose pieces to the skillet and turn the heat to very low. Cover and cook (the mixture should be bubbling, but barely) for at least 2 hours, turning only once or twice, until the goose is very tender. Add

(continued)

the vinegar, sliced fresh fruit, and a good grinding of black pepper, and cook, covered, stirring occasionally, until the fruit is tender, 10 to 15 minutes. Remove and discard the bay leaves. Taste, adjust the seasoning, and serve.

roasted new potatoes
with rosemary

Classic and easy, as long as you remember it's better to overcook the potatoes than undercook them.

MAKES 6 TO 8 SERVINGS

TIME: 45 MINUTES

3 pounds new potatoes, the smaller the better, washed and dried

3 tablespoons extra virgin olive oil

1 tablespoon fresh rosemary leaves, or 1 teaspoon dried

12 garlic cloves, unpeeled, optional

Salt and freshly ground black pepper

1. Preheat the oven to 425°F. Put the potatoes in an ovenproof casserole or saucepan and toss with all the remaining ingredients. Cover and roast, shaking the pan occasionally, until the potatoes are tender, 30 to 45 minutes.

2. Uncover, stir once or twice, and serve.

cranberry clafouti

The clafouti is essentially a fruit-laden pancake. I love this Americanized version, which is crunchy and sweet.

MAKES 6 TO 8 SERVINGS

TIME: 1 HOUR

1 tablespoon unsalted butter, more or less, for greasing the pan

1 cup sugar

2 eggs

1 cup all-purpose flour

1 cup half-and-half or whole milk

Pinch of salt

2 cups fresh cranberries

1 scant cup walnuts

Confectioners' sugar

1. Preheat the oven to 425°F. Butter a 9- or 10-inch round deep pie plate or porcelain dish, or a gratin dish of similar size. Sprinkle it with a tablespoon or so of the sugar, then swirl the dish to coat it evenly with the sugar; invert to remove the excess.

2. Beat the eggs well, then add the remaining sugar; beat until smooth. Add the flour and beat again until smooth. Add the half-and-half and salt and beat once more until smooth.

3. Coarsely chop the cranberries and walnuts; you can do this in a food processor if you like, but be careful not to overprocess—you want to break up the cranberries, not mince them. Put the cranberry-nut mixture in the bottom of the dish and pour the batter over it.

4. Bake for 20 to 30 minutes, or until the clafouti is nicely browned on top and a knife inserted into it comes out clean. Sift some confectioners' sugar over it and serve warm or at room temperature.

a crowd-pleasing mexican buffet

SHRIMP "SEVICHE"

FISH TACOS WITH FRESH SALSA

CHICKEN THIGHS WITH MEXICAN FLAVORS

LIME GRANITA (PAGE 57)

For some reason, home-cooked Mexican-style food
has a reputation for being difficult (at least when you get
beyond the standard tacos). But there's a great deal of variety,
and much of it has wide appeal, even to kids.

KEYS TO SUCCESS

- If you can get fresh shrimp (it's not common, but is found locally in season), which is usually small, sweet, and delicious, this is the place to use it.

- In the fish tacos, substitute freely for the cod—you can use any white-fleshed fish, like sea bass, red snapper, halibut, and so on, or steak fish like swordfish or shark.

- It's usually possible to buy boned chicken thighs, but if you cannot you have two choices: Bone them yourself—it's easy and intuitive—or cook the chicken with the bones in.

- If you like, round out this menu with Coconut Rice and Beans (page 120).

WINE

A simple, crisp, inexpensive white—Muscadet, Graves, or Pinot Grigio, for example—will do well here, but so will good beer.

THE TIMETABLE

- Marinate the chicken if you have time. Start the granita, then make the salsa.

- Do the slicing and dicing for the tacos and chicken; prepare the "seviche."

- Grill the chicken, which can be served at room temperature; finally, cook the fish. Serve everything at once, or in courses.

shrimp "seviche"

Not a true seviche, because the shrimp is cooked first; but it has the right flavors, bright and slightly hot.

MAKES 8 SERVINGS

TIME: 15 MINUTES

2 pounds small shrimp, peeled

6 limes

1 tablespoon olive oil

1 ripe tomato, cored, seeded, and diced

$1/2$ cup minced white or red onion

1 garlic clove, minced

1 jalapeño, minced (or use crushed red pepper flakes or any other source of heat), or to taste

Salt and freshly ground black pepper

1 cup cilantro, chopped

1. Cook the shrimp however is convenient: You can steam them above boiling water, immerse them in boiling water, or microwave them; in any case, the cooking time will be just a few minutes. Chill (if you're in a hurry, run the shrimp under cold water).

2. Quarter two of the limes and set aside; juice the remaining limes. Combine the lime juice with the oil, tomato, onion, garlic, chile, and shrimp. Toss and add salt and pepper to taste, along with more chile if you like. Stir in about half the cilantro, then top with the rest. Serve with the lime wedges and with tortilla chips.

fish tacos with fresh salsa

The fish taco, a rarity on the East Coast, breathes new life into the "sandwich" of Mexico and the Southwest, replacing mystery meat with an identifiable fillet of delicate white fish like cod. Instead of frying, as is common in tacquerias, *I like to steam the fish in its own juices, which can be done on top of the stove or in a microwave oven.*

MAKES 8 SERVINGS

TIME: 20 MINUTES

1 large onion, roughly chopped

2 jalapeños, stemmed and roughly chopped

3 pounds fillet of cod or other thick white fish (see Keys to Success)

Salt and freshly ground black pepper

Twenty-four 6-inch corn tortillas, or sixteen 12-inch corn or flour tortillas

Fresh Salsa (recipe follows)

Hot sauce or chile paste, optional

Sour cream or grated cheese, optional

Chopped lettuce, tomatoes, and cucumbers, optional

Cilantro sprigs, optional

Lime wedges

1. Put the onion and jalapeños in the bottom of a large nonstick skillet (or, if you prefer, a microwavable casserole). Add a tablespoon of water and top with the fish; sprinkle with salt and pepper. Cover the skillet (or casserole) and put the pan over medium heat (or the casserole in the microwave). Cook for about 6 minutes (3 for the microwave, on "high"), or until the fish is done (it will be opaque throughout).

2. While the fish is cooking, heat the tortillas. You can dry-toast them in a skillet, one at a time; just flip once or twice, over medium heat, until hot, a minute or so. Or heat them in a microwave: wrap half a dozen in a just slightly damp towel and nuke on high for about a minute.

3. To serve, put a portion of fish (along with a bit of its onion and jalapeño) and some of the salsa in a warm tortilla; add as many of the optional ingredients as you like. Squeeze a bit of lime juice over all.

fresh salsa

MAKES ABOUT 2 CUPS

TIME: 20 MINUTES

12 plum tomatoes

1 large white onion, chopped

2 garlic cloves, minced

1 tablespoon chili powder, or to taste

Salt

1 cup cilantro leaves, chopped

Not only is this inarguably better than store-bought salsa, eventually you'll develop a style and make it your own.

1. Broil the tomatoes, as close to the heat source as you can get them, until blistered and a little blackened, 5 to 10 minutes.

2. Put them in a blender, skins and all, with the onion, garlic, chili powder, and a big pinch of salt. Whiz until chunky, pour into a bowl, and then stir in the cilantro by hand. This is best used right away, but will retain decent flavor, refrigerated, for a day or two.

chicken thighs
with mexican flavors

The dark, rich meat of a chicken thigh responds brilliantly to the strong, equatorial flavors most closely associated with grilling. This Mexican-style treatment packs plenty of punch, even if you use the minimum amount of cayenne (as I do), or omit it entirely.

MAKES 8 SERVINGS

TIME: 30 TO 60 MINUTES

8 garlic cloves

1 large onion, quartered

2 tablespoons fresh oregano leaves, or 1 teaspoon dried

1 tablespoon ground cumin

$1/2$ teaspoon cayenne, or to taste

Pinch of ground cloves

Salt and freshly ground black pepper

2 tablespoons peanut or other oil

$1/4$ cup orange juice, preferably freshly squeezed

$1/4$ cup fresh lime juice

About 3 pounds boneless chicken thighs, or 4 pounds bone-in thighs

Minced cilantro

1. Preheat a gas grill or start a wood or charcoal fire, or preheat the broiler; the fire should be moderately hot, and the rack at least 4 inches from the heat source. Combine the garlic, onion, oregano, cumin, cayenne, cloves, salt, pepper, and oil in a blender or small food processor and blend until fairly smooth. Add the juices, then taste and adjust the seasoning; the blend should be powerful.

2. Smear this mixture all over the chicken; if time allows, marinate the chicken for 30 minutes or so. Grill or broil 6 to 8 minutes per side, watching carefully, until the meat is nicely browned on the outside and cooked through on the inside (bone-in thighs will take longer, about 20 minutes total). Serve hot or at room temperature, garnished with the cilantro.

a feast for seafood lovers

CHILE-FRIED SHRIMP WITH SCALLIONS AND ORANGE

BOUILLABAISSE

BREAD

TUNA AU POIVRE

SIMPLE GREEN SALAD (PAGE 69)

FREE-FORM APPLE OR PEAR TART (PAGE 237)

This menu draws inspiration from all over the world, and is best served as a semi-elegant sit-down dinner. Eliminate the tuna dish, however, and it will make a fine buffet.

KEYS TO SUCCESS

- If you have an adventuresome group, you can serve the shrimp with only tail and feelers removed, leaving the rest of the peel on. It's edible and adds both crunch and flavor.

- The key to Bouillabaisse is a variety of good fish of different types, so use this recipe as a set of guidelines rather than strict dogma and don't worry about duplicating the exact types or quantities of fish.

- For a cross-cultural twist, substitute Broiled Bluefish or Mackerel with Green Tea Salt (page 153), for the tuna.

WINE

The shrimp dish is a spicy wine killer, so you might want to start with Champagne. After that, switch to a rosé or light red for the Bouillabaisse (or keep drinking Champagne), and finally a powerful Cabernet or Bordeaux for the tuna, which has more in common with good steak than any other fish. Or drink rosé all the way through.

THE TIMETABLE

This is more challenging than most of the menus in this book, but it's still manageable by one person in a reasonable amount of time.

- First, ready the ingredients for the tart (you can even roll out the dough and refrigerate it) and salad, then complete Step 1 of the Bouillabaisse.

- Get the components for the tuna ready, then cook and serve the shrimp. While that's being cleared, add the fish to the Bouillabaisse; it only takes about 20 minutes from that point until completion. Preheat the oven for the tuna.

- After the Bouillabaisse is eaten, prepare the tuna and salad; this isn't a long procedure either, once you're set up.

- After eating the main course, assemble and bake the tart.

chile-fried shrimp with scallions and orange

How nicely the flavors of chiles and oranges complement one another in this dish, essentially an easy stir-fry. Note that you want fairly large pieces of orange, so stick with a vegetable peeler or paring knife; avoid as much of the bitter white pith as you can without getting obsessive about it.

MAKES 8 SERVINGS

TIME: 20 MINUTES

2 oranges or large tangerines

2 tablespoons peanut or vegetable oil

4 or more small dried chiles, or to taste

3 pounds shrimp, peeled

Salt and freshly ground black pepper

16 scallions, trimmed and cut into 2-inch lengths

Sesame seeds for garnish

I. Use a vegetable peeler to remove the zest from the oranges; roughly chop the zest. Cut the oranges and juice them; set the juice aside.

2. Put a large skillet over medium-high heat and add the oil. A minute later, add the chiles and orange zest. After a minute or two the chiles will start smoking; turn the heat to high and add the shrimp. Cook without stirring for about 2 minutes, then stir the shrimp and season with salt and pepper.

3. Add the scallions and cook, stirring occasionally, just until they begin to soften, about 2 minutes. Stir in the orange juice. Taste and adjust the seasoning if necessary, garnish with the sesame seeds, and serve.

bouillabaisse

Bouillabaisse, the Mediterranean fish stew that is more difficult to spell than to prepare, is traditionally neither an idée fixe *nor the centerpiece of a* grande bouffe, *but a spur-of-the-moment combination of the day's catch.*

MAKES 8 SERVINGS

TIME: 1 HOUR

1 tablespoon olive oil

2 medium onions, roughly chopped

2 navel or other oranges

2 teaspoons fennel seeds

Big pinch of saffron, optional

1 dried chile, or a pinch of cayenne, or to taste

2 cups chopped fresh or canned tomatoes

1 to 1½ pounds monkfish, catfish, or blackfish, cut into 1-inch cubes

3 pounds hard-shell (littleneck) clams, cockles, or mussels, well washed

1 to 1½ pounds shrimp or scallops, cut into bite-sized pieces if necessary

1 to 1½ pounds cod or other delicate white-fleshed fish, cut into 6 large chunks

1 tablespoon minced garlic

1 cup roughly chopped fresh parsley

1. Put the olive oil in a casserole or large saucepan over medium heat. Add the onions and cook, stirring occasionally, until softened, about 5 minutes. Meanwhile, use a vegetable peeler to strip the zest from the oranges (save the oranges themselves for another use). Add the zest, fennel, saffron, if you're using it, and chile and cook for about a minute. Add the tomatoes and turn the heat to medium-high. When the mixture boils, reduce the heat to medium, and cook, stirring occasionally, until the mixture becomes saucelike, 10 to 15 minutes. (You can prepare the dish several hours in advance up to this point; cover and set aside until you're ready to eat.)

2. Add the monkfish and raise the heat to medium-high. When the mixture begins to boil, reduce the heat to medium-low and cook, stirring occasionally, until it is just about tender, 10 minutes or so.

3. Add the clams, raise the heat to high, and stir; when the mixture boils, reduce the heat to low, cover, and cook until the clams begin to open, 5 to 10 minutes. (Any clams that do not open can be pried open at the table with a butter knife.) Add the shrimp and white fish, stir, and cover; cook, stirring gently once or twice, until the white fish is just about done (a thin-

(continued)

bladed knife will pierce it with little resistance), about 5 minutes. (If the mixture is very thick—there should be some broth—add a cup or so of hot water.) Stir in the garlic and cook 1 minute more. Stir in the parsley and serve with crusty bread.

tuna au poivre

Tuna au Poivre is yet another recipe that plays on tuna's similarity to beefsteak. How finely to grind the pepper is a matter of taste. Mine dictates "coarsely ground" as opposed to "cracked." That is, ground to the point where there are no large pieces left, but not to the point of powder. The coarser the grind, the more powerful the result will taste. It's worth using a (clean) coffee or spice grinder to do the grinding (see page 153); if you're grinding by hand 4 tablespoons is going to take you a while.

MAKES 8 SERVINGS

TIME: 30 MINUTES

4 tablespoons coarsely ground black pepper

2 tablespoons extra virgin olive oil

Four 8- to 10-ounce tuna steaks, each at least 1 inch thick

Salt

4 tablespoons ($^1/_2$ stick) unsalted butter or use more oil

$^1/_2$ cup minced shallots

$1^1/_2$ cups dry red wine

1. Preheat the oven to 500°F; put the pepper on a flat plate. Place a large skillet, preferably nonstick, over medium-high heat; add the olive oil. Dredge both sides of each piece of tuna lightly in the pepper; it will adhere nicely, forming a thin coat. (Use a bit more pepper if necessary.) As they're dredged, add the steaks to the pan (if you must use two pans, double the amount of oil); when they are all in, turn the heat to high. Cook about 2 minutes, then turn; add salt, then cook another 1 minute. Turn heat to low, remove steaks to an ovenproof plate, and place in the oven.

2. Add half the butter to the pan (if you used two pans to brown the tuna, just use one to make the sauce), followed by the shallots. Lower the heat to medium, and cook, stirring, until the shallots soften, about 2 minutes. Raise the heat to medium-high and add the wine; let it bubble away for a minute or so and add the remaining butter. Cook, stirring occasionally, until the butter melts and the sauce is thickened.

3. By this time the tuna will be medium-rare (cut into one to make certain). Cut the steaks in half, put each serving on a plate, and spoon a little sauce over it.

a quick, light asian meal

CURRIED MUSSELS

SIMMERED TOFU WITH GROUND PORK (MA-PO TOFU)

EASY RICE

COCONUT SORBET

A great deal of Asian food is quick to prepare, and no less delicious for that. Start with a steamed mussel dish that is a far cry from the familiar Mediterranean preparation, continue with a superior homemade version of a Chinese restaurant standard, and finish with my all-time favorite sorbet.

KEYS TO SUCCESS

- Wild mussels are more flavorful (and, usually, less expensive) than farm-raised, but they're harder to clean. Given that you're adding curry to this dish, I would go with farm-raised if you're given a choice.

- Soft or silken tofu is best here—handle either gently—but if you can find only firm tofu, that's not a problem.

- If you're looking for a green to add to this menu, think about Herbed Green Salad with Soy Vinaigrette (page 38).

WINE

Champagne is the typical cop-out (I'm as guilty as anyone) when serving Asian food, and it's beautiful here. But a fruity but fairly dry Riesling or Gewürztraminer would do equally well.

THE TIMETABLE

- Wash the mussels and set them up in the pot, but don't turn on the heat.

- Get everything ready for the tofu and start the rice. Just before the action really begins, combine the ingredients for the sorbet.

- Cook and eat the mussels. While the table is being cleared, make the tofu. Just before sitting down to eat it and the rice, start the ice cream machine for the sorbet. (If you have a hand-cranked machine, make the sorbet in advance.)

curried mussels

Whenever you clean mussels, discard any with broken shells. If the mussels have beards—the hairy vegetative growth that is attached to the shell—trim them off. Wash the mussels well, then cook them. Any that do not open are still safe to eat; just pry them open with a dull knife.

MAKES 8 SERVINGS

TIME: 30 MINUTES

3 shallots, peeled and minced

6 pounds mussels, trimmed of their beards and well washed

$^1/_2$ cup dry white wine

2 tablespoons curry powder

$^1/_4$ cup fresh lime juice

Salt and freshly ground black pepper

1. Combine the shallots, mussels, wine, and curry powder in a large, heavy saucepan and turn the heat to high. Cook, shaking the pan occasionally, just until the mussels open, about 10 minutes.

2. Turn off the heat and remove the mussels with a slotted spoon or strainer. Add the lime juice, turn the heat to medium, and stir to blend. Add salt and pepper, taste and adjust the seasoning, then return the mussels to the pot and stir to reheat. Serve, spooning the broth over the mussels.

simmered tofu with ground pork (ma-po tofu)

This is not a stir-fry, but a simmered dish, easy and fast. The cooking time totals about 10 minutes, and the preparation time is about the same, so make sure to start the rice first.

MAKES 8 SERVINGS

TIME: 20 MINUTES

2 tablespoons peanut or other oil

2 tablespoons minced garlic

2 tablespoons minced ginger

$1/4$ teaspoon crushed red pepper flakes, or to taste

$1/2$ pound ground pork

1 cup chopped scallions, green part only

1 cup stock or water

2 pounds soft or silken tofu, cut into $1/2$-inch cubes

$1/4$ cup soy sauce

Salt

Minced cilantro, optional

1. Put the oil in a deep 12-inch skillet or wok, preferably nonstick, and turn the heat to medium-high. A minute later, add the garlic, ginger, and red pepper flakes and cook just until they begin to sizzle, less than a minute. Add the pork and stir to break it up; cook, stirring occasionally, until it loses most of its pink color.

2. Add the scallions and stir; add the stock. Cook for a minute or so, scraping the bottom of the pan with a wooden spoon if necessary to loosen any stuck bits of meat, then add the tofu. Cook, stirring once or twice, until the tofu is heated through, about 2 minutes.

3. Stir in the soy sauce, taste, and add salt and additional red pepper flakes as necessary. Garnish with the cilantro, if you like, and serve.

easy rice

A Chinese method for making rice, and not only foolproof but quite flexible. It will hold up to an hour.

MAKES 8 SERVINGS

TIME: ABOUT 20 MINUTES

3 cups long-, medium-, or short-grain rice, rinsed and drained

5 cups water

2 teaspoons salt, or to taste

1. Combine all the ingredients in a medium saucepan and bring to a boil over medium-high heat. When the water starts boiling, stir and turn the heat down to medium, so that it still bubbles but not furiously.

2. In 8 to 12 minutes small craters will appear on the surface of the rice, indicating that the water is almost all absorbed. Cover the pot, turn the heat to low, and cook until tender, about 5 more minutes. Serve immediately or let the rice sit for up to an hour, over the lowest possible heat, before serving.

coconut sorbet

If you have an ice cream machine, this is one of the fastest, easiest, most satisfying desserts you can make.

MAKES 1 QUART

TIME: 5 MINUTES, PLUS TIME TO FREEZE

3 cans coconut milk, about
32 ounces

1 cup sugar, or to taste

2 teaspoons vanilla extract

1. Combine the coconut milk with the sugar and taste; add more sugar if you like. Add the vanilla and stir.

2. Freeze in an ice cream machine according to the instructions. Serve as soon as possible after making, or freeze and let "warm" in the refrigerator for 30 minutes before serving. Best the day it is made.

a mediterranean dinner

FIGS STUFFED WITH GOAT CHEESE

CANAPÉS WITH PIQUILLO PEPPERS AND ANCHOVIES

PASTA WITH WALNUTS

LAMB STEW WITH DILL

CITRUS WITH HONEY AND MINT (PAGE 103)

Arguably, this is not strictly Mediterranean—piquillo peppers
come from an inland part of Spain closer to the Atlantic—
but the spirit is here. It's warm, simple, and inviting, a perfect
meal for chilly weather.

KEYS TO SUCCESS

- Fresh figs may be green or dark purple; the color does not affect the flavor (ripeness and variety do), but most people perceive purple figs as more attractive.

- For the stew, the best cut of meat is lamb shoulder. In some supermarkets (and at most butcher counters), you will be able to find boneless shoulder, perhaps even already cut into chunks. If you can't, buy shoulder lamb chops, the thickest you can find, and cut them up yourself, discarding any hard pieces of white fat.

WINE

A fruity red is in order, but nothing spectacular is needed: Perhaps a
Côtes du Rhone blend, or a Chianti Classico.

THE TIMETABLE

- Make the dessert as far in advance as you like, up to a day ahead or even two. (Keep it covered and refrigerated.)

- Start with the stew, finishing it with the exception of the final addition of peas, scallions, and dill. Not only can you keep it warm, you can refrigerate and reheat it should you choose to do so.

- Make the appetizers an hour or so before your guests arrive.

- The pasta is fast, and pretty much a last-minute thing; you can make it while your guests munch on the starters, or even a little later.

figs stuffed with goat cheese

Fall is the time for fresh figs, which people who live in Mediterranean climates (this includes many Californians) take for granted but are a real treat for the rest of us.

MAKES 8 SERVINGS

TIME: 15 MINUTES

4 to 6 ounces soft, fresh goat cheese

1 tablespoon good balsamic vinegar

16 fresh figs, washed and drained

1. Use your fingers to roll the goat cheese into 32 small balls, each $1/2$ inch or less in diameter. Place them on a plate and drizzle with the vinegar. Shake the plate gently to coat the cheese balls evenly.

2. Cut the figs in half and press a cheese ball into the center of each. As the figs are stuffed, return them, stuffed side up, to the plate where the cheese was marinating. Serve within an hour.

canapés with piquillo peppers and anchovies

Piquillo peppers are wood-roasted peppers from Spain, sold in cans or jars. If you cannot find them, substitute homemade roasted peppers (see page 113) or canned "pimientos."

MAKES 8 SERVINGS

TIME: 20 MINUTES

Eight ³/4-inch-thick (roughly) slices French or Italian bread, cut in half

1 teaspoon minced garlic

8 piquillo peppers, cut in half (or 4 or 5 roasted peppers)

16 anchovies, oil reserved

Extra virgin olive oil, optional

1. Lightly toast the bread. Top each piece with a tiny bit of garlic, then layer with a piece of piquillo and an anchovy. Drizzle with a little anchovy oil and/or olive oil if you're using it.

2. Serve within an hour.

pasta with walnuts

You might think of this as winter pesto, with a higher percentage of walnuts and the always-available parsley filling in for summer's basil—though if you can find good basil, by all means use it.

MAKES 8 SERVINGS

TIME: 20 MINUTES

2 cups walnut or pecan halves

1 cup loosely packed fresh parsley or basil leaves

2 garlic cloves

1 cup extra virgin olive oil, plus more if needed

Salt and freshly ground black pepper

2 pounds linguine, spaghetti, or other long pasta

1. Bring a large pot of water to a boil and salt it. Meanwhile, combine the nuts, parsley, and garlic in a small food processor and turn the machine on (or use a mortar and pestle). With the machine running, add the oil gradually, using just enough so that the mixture forms a creamy paste. Season to taste with salt and pepper.

2. Cook the pasta, stirring occasionally, until it is tender but not mushy. When it is ready, drain it—reserve some of the cooking water—and toss with the sauce; if the mixture appears too thick, thin with a little of the pasta cooking water (or more olive oil). Serve.

lamb stew with dill

The smaller the pieces you cut, the shorter the cooking time, but I wouldn't make them too small or you'll rob yourself of some of the satisfaction of eating them.

MAKES 8 SERVINGS

TIME: 1 TO 1½ HOURS, LARGELY UNATTENDED

3 pounds boneless lamb, from the shoulder, cut into roughly 1½-inch chunks

8 shallots

16 to 24 very small new potatoes, washed

Salt and freshly ground black pepper

4 carrots, diced into roughly pea-size bits, optional

2 cups green peas (frozen are okay)

16 scallions, optional

1 cup snipped dill leaves, or more

8 lemon wedges

1. Put the lamb in a large skillet over high heat; let the meat sear, undisturbed, for about 4 minutes, or until the underside is nicely browned (don't worry if not all of the pieces brown). Stir, then add the shallots and potatoes. Let cook another couple of minutes, then add salt, pepper, and 1½ cups water. Stir, scraping the bottom if necessary to loosen any bits of meat that may have stuck. Turn the heat to low, cover, and let the mixture simmer for about 45 minutes, stirring once or twice during that period.

2. Uncover and add the carrots, if you're using them; stir once, re-cover, and let simmer for about 15 minutes more, or until the lamb and potatoes are tender.

3. Uncover and add the peas and scallions, if you're using. Raise the heat if necessary to boil away excess liquid. Taste and adjust the seasoning, then serve, each plate garnished with some of the dill and accompanied by a lemon wedge.

a simple sit-down

CARROT, SPINACH, AND RICE STEW

COD WITH CHICKPEAS AND SHERRY

BREAD

BAKED PEARS

These are simple dishes, but Old World classics
nevertheless—delicious peasant food. Together, they make for a
pleasant, informal menu that you can share with anyone.

KEYS TO SUCCESS

- The vegetable stew is a little thicker than a soup, but still eaten with a spoon; it is designed to be a starter, not a side dish. If you would rather have a side dish, make Golden Pilaf (page 140) instead.

- Canned chickpeas do not have as much flavor as cooked dried chickpeas, but they are incomparably more convenient, as dried chickpeas can take 3 hours to soften. Your choice.

- Look for large pears, just about ripe; their "shoulders" should yield to gentle pressure, but they should not be mushy.

WINE

Any fairly light red, from Beaujolais to a wine
from southern France or a similar California blend.

THE TIMETABLE

- If you are using dried chickpeas, get a head start on them; you can reduce their cooking time a bit by soaking them overnight, but it isn't necessary.

- Once those are done, you can assemble the whole meal in less than 90 minutes. Start with the stew, which can be reheated any time (if it becomes too thick, add a little more water or stock). When it's done, begin the fish.

- Put the pears in the oven when you begin eating; they're best when served warm, not hot.

carrot, spinach, and rice stew

This is a stew of carrots, spinach, and rice cooked, you might say, to death. I first ate it at a Turkish lunch counter, and was taken by its depth of flavor. The whole is definitely greater than the sum of its parts.

MAKES 8 SERVINGS

TIME: 45 MINUTES

1 pound carrots, cut into $^1/4$-inch dice

$1^1/2$ cups long-grain rice, preferably basmati

Salt

2 pounds fresh spinach, thick stems removed and discarded, thoroughly washed and roughly chopped

6 garlic cloves, minced, optional

4 tablespoons ($^1/2$ stick) unsalted butter, optional

Freshly ground black pepper

1. Combine the carrots with 6 cups of water in a large saucepan and turn the heat to high. Bring to a boil, then stir in the rice and a large pinch of salt. When the mixture returns to the boil, add the spinach, then adjust the heat so that it simmers gently.

2. Cook, stirring occasionally, until the rice and carrots are very tender, about 30 minutes, and the mixture takes on the consistency of a thick stew. When it reaches this stage, stir in the garlic and/or butter, if you're using either or both, and cook another 5 minutes. Add pepper, taste and adjust the seasoning, and serve.

cod with chickpeas and sherry

An Andalusian dish with a sweet, aromatic sauce.

MAKES 8 SERVINGS

TIME: 30 MINUTES WITH COOKED OR
CANNED CHICKPEAS

6 tablespoons olive oil

4 cod fillets, each about 1 inch
thick, about 3 pounds total

Salt and freshly ground black
pepper

6 cups cooked chickpeas (or
canned), with 1 cup reserved
cooking liquid

1^1/$_2$ cups sherry, preferably
amontillado

^{1}/$_4$ cup minced garlic

Chopped fresh parsley, optional

1. Preheat the oven to 300°F. Put 3 tablespoons of the oil in a nonstick skillet large enough to hold the cod in one layer (cook in batches if necessary, but under-cook the first batch by about a minute, as it will remain in the oven longer, and use more oil if necessary); turn the heat to medium-high. When the oil is hot, add the fish, skin (it won't have skin, but will be shiny) side up. Cook, undisturbed, for about 5 minutes, or until the cooked side is evenly browned. Turn the fish onto an ovenproof plate, browned side up, sprinkle with salt and pepper, and put it in the oven.

2. Immediately add the chickpeas (with about 1 cup of their liquid) to the skillet and cook, stirring, for about a minute. Add all but 2 tablespoons of the sherry and raise the heat to high. Cook, shaking the pan now and then, until the liquid is all but evaporated and the chickpeas are beginning to brown, about 10 minutes. Stir in the garlic along with some salt and pepper and cook 1 minute, stirring occasionally; stir in the remaining olive oil and sherry.

3. By this time the fish will be done. (A thin-bladed knife inserted into it should meet no resistance. If it is not done, hold the chickpeas over low heat until it is.) Serve the fish on top of the chickpeas, garnished with the parsley, if you like.

baked pears

Serve these, if you like, with a dollop of sweetened whipped cream, ice cream, or sour cream.

MAKES 8 SERVINGS

TIME: 45 MINUTES

4 large pears, peeled, halved, and cored

8 teaspoons unsalted butter

8 teaspoons brown sugar

1. Preheat the oven to 350°F. Place the pears, cavities up, in a baking pan filmed with a little water.

2. Fill the cavities with a teaspoon each of butter and sugar. Cover the pan. After about 15 minutes of cooking, brush the surface of the pears with the butter-sugar mixture, which will have softened. Bake until very soft, about 30 minutes; serve warm or at room temperature.

winter

a cocktail party

PROSCIUTTO, FIG, AND PARMESAN ROLLS (PAGE 132)

WHITE BEAN DIP

SKEWERED CRISP SHIITAKES WITH GARLIC

MISO-BROILED SCALLOPS

FENNEL, ORANGE, AND APPLE SKEWERS

This is a plan for a stand-up cocktail party, eclectic and fun.
All of these dishes would make great starters for regular sit-down
meals, or as part of a buffet.

KEYS TO SUCCESS

- If it is winter, you should be able to find true bay scallops (usually called Nantucket bays), especially if you live in the Northeast. They are worth the extra cost.

- Miso, fermented soybean paste from Japan, is a complex and delicious substance available in many styles. If you have a choice, go for a dark "red" (actually brown) miso.

- Crispy Pork Bits with Jerk Seasonings (page 119), cut into small pieces, is also great stand-up food.

WINE

Champagne, or cocktails, or both white and red wines.

THE TIMETABLE

- The prosciutto rolls and bean dip can be made in advance. Serve those first, too.

- About 30 minutes before serving them, start the shiitakes, and pass them next.

- As they're going around, prepare the scallops.

- Finish with the fruit skewers.

white bean dip

For a great additional surprise, add some lemon zest to the food processor for the last 10 seconds or so.

MAKES 8 SERVINGS

TIME: 10 MINUTES (WITH PRECOOKED OR CANNED BEANS)

About 2 cups white beans, drained but quite moist

1 or 2 garlic cloves

Salt

3 tablespoons plus 2 teaspoons extra virgin olive oil

2 teaspoons minced fresh rosemary or thyme, or
2 teaspoons ground cumin

Freshly ground black pepper

A rosemary or thyme sprig, optional

1. Put the beans in the container of a food processor with the garlic and some salt. Turn the machine on and add the 3 tablespoons olive oil in a steady stream through the feed tube; process until the mixture is smooth. Taste and adjust the seasoning, then cover and refrigerate (up to 2 days) until about an hour before you're ready to serve.

2. Just before serving, stir in the herbs and some pepper, drizzle with the remaining olive oil, and garnish with the herb sprig, if you like. Serve with chips, cut-up raw vegetables, or both.

skewered crisp shiitakes with garlic

One of the great advances of the modern supermarket was the appearance of fresh shiitake mushrooms on a regular basis.

MAKES 20 SKEWERS,

ENOUGH FOR 8 TO 10

TIME: ABOUT 1 HOUR

---

40 shiitake caps, about 1 pound (stems should be reserved for stock or discarded)

$1/3$ cup extra virgin olive oil

1 tablespoon chopped garlic

Salt and freshly ground black pepper

1. Preheat the oven to 450°F. Put the shiitakes in one layer in a roasting pan and add the olive oil. Roast for about 20 minutes, until the shiitakes have begun to shrink. Stir in the garlic, salt, and pepper and return to the oven, tossing and turning occasionally, until the shiitakes are crisp, another 20 minutes or so.

2. Cool slightly, then skewer the mushrooms on toothpicks. Serve warm.

miso-broiled scallops

An appetizer that brilliantly displays the complexity of miso.

MAKES 8 SERVINGS

TIME: 20 MINUTES, OR MORE

3/4 cup miso

3 tablespoons mirin, fruity white wine, or dry white wine

1 cup minced onion

Salt and cayenne

2 pounds scallops

Juice of 1 lime

1. Preheat a broiler or grill, setting the rack as close as possible to the heat source. Put the miso in a bowl, add the mirin, and whisk until smooth. Stir in the onion, a little bit of salt, and a pinch of cayenne. Add the scallops and let them marinate while the broiler or grill preheats; or refrigerate for up to a day.

2. Broil until lightly browned, without turning, 2 to 3 minutes, or grill, turning once after a minute or two. Sprinkle with the lime juice and serve with toothpicks.

fennel, orange, and apple skewers

Not quite dessert, but juicy and refreshing.

MAKES 20 SKEWERS,
ENOUGH FOR 8 TO 10
TIME: 20 MINUTES

^{1}/2 fennel bulb

2 or 3 clementines, tangerines, or oranges

2 Granny Smith apples

Juice of 1 lemon

20 fresh mint leaves

1. Cut the fennel into twenty small pieces. Segment the clementines or cut up the oranges; you need twenty pieces. Peel and cut twenty small pieces of apple; toss them with the lemon juice immediately.

2. Use toothpicks to spear a piece of fennel, then clementine, then mint, and finally apple. Serve within 30 minutes.

a hearty midwinter sit-down

MUSHROOM-BARLEY SOUP

BREADED LAMB CUTLETS

PILAF WITH PINE NUTS AND CURRANTS

TENDER SPINACH AND CRISP SHALLOTS

MAPLE BREAD PUDDING (PAGE 250)

This is a big meal, rich and filling, a feast of irresistible
peasant food that can be served easily and attractively. It's
the kind of meal where people will eat too much,
but we all deserve those once in a while.

KEYS TO SUCCESS

- Try to find dried porcini sold in bulk, not in tiny little packages of less than an ounce each (these are a complete rip-off). If you live in a big city, a major Italian or specialty food market will have them; otherwise, you can find good sources on the Internet.

- Basmati rice is probably the best for pilaf, but if you don't have it use any long-grain rice.

- If it's late winter, bordering on spring, think about substituting Pan-Roasted Asparagus Soup with Tarragon (page 18).

WINE

Red, and good. I always like Cabernet with lamb, and it can be
an austere specimen from Bordeaux or a relatively fruity choice from
California. Rioja would be great here, too.

THE TIMETABLE

- Bread pudding and soup first; the latter can be reheated when you're ready to serve.

- Fry the shallots and set them aside. Get all the ingredients ready for the lamb and spinach. An hour or so before serving the main course, start the pilaf and hold it warm over a very low flame when it's ready.

- After serving the soup, you're going to need to spend a little while in the kitchen to sauté the lamb and finish the spinach.

mushroom-barley soup

A good Mushroom-Barley Soup doesn't necessarily need meat. You can make it with dried porcini, which can be reconstituted in hot water in less than 10 minutes, giving you not only the best-tasting mushrooms you can find outside of the woods but an intensely flavored broth that rivals beef stock. A touch of soy sauce is untraditional but really enhances the flavor.

MAKES 8 SERVINGS

TIME: 45 MINUTES

1 1/2 ounces dried porcini mushrooms, about 1 1/2 cups

1/4 cup olive oil

1/2 pound shiitake or button (white) mushrooms, stemmed and roughly chopped (stems should be reserved for stock or discarded)

4 medium carrots, sliced

1 1/2 cups pearled barley

Salt and freshly ground black pepper

1 bay leaf

2 tablespoons soy sauce

1. Soak the porcini in 4 cups very hot water. Put the olive oil in a medium saucepan and turn the heat to high. Add the shiitakes and carrots. Cook, stirring occasionally, until they begin to brown. Add the barley and continue to cook, stirring frequently, until it begins to brown; sprinkle with a little salt and pepper. Remove the porcini from their soaking liquid, but do *not* discard the liquid; sort through and discard hard bits, if any.

2. Add the porcini to the pot and cook, stirring, for about a minute. Add the bay leaf, the strained mushroom soaking water, and 5 cups additional water (or stock, if you prefer). Bring to a boil, then lower the heat to a simmer; cook until the barley is very tender, 20 to 30 minutes. If the soup is very thick, add a little more water. Add the soy sauce, then taste and add more salt if necessary and plenty of pepper. Remove and discard the bay leaf. Serve hot.

breaded lamb cutlets

Though it may seem surprising, in many ways lamb is the meat most suited to this simple treatment. Like all cutlet preparations, it's lightning-quick.

MAKES 8 SERVINGS

TIME: 20 MINUTES

Sixteen 1-inch-thick medallions of lamb, cut from 2 racks, or from the loin or leg

4 tablespoons extra virgin olive oil

3 eggs

Panko (Japanese bread crumbs) or other bread crumbs for dredging

Salt and freshly ground black pepper

2 teaspoons ground cumin, optional, or use about
1 tablespoon fresh or 1 teaspoon dried rosemary

Chopped fresh parsley, optional

2 lemons, cut into wedges

1. Preheat the oven to 200°F. If you're using rib or loin slices, pound them lightly with the heel of your hand until they are about $1/2$ inch thick. If you're using leg, put them between two pieces of wax paper or plastic wrap and pound with a mallet or rolling pin until they are about $1/2$ inch thick. Put a nonstick or well-seasoned skillet over medium-high heat and add the oil. Beat the eggs and put the bread crumbs on a plate.

2. When the oil shimmers, dip a lamb medallion in the egg, and press both sides into the bread crumbs. Add to the skillet; do not crowd—you will have to cook in batches. When the meat is in the skillet, season it with salt and pepper, and sprinkle it with a pinch of cumin or rosemary, if you like.

3. As the meat browns, flip it and brown the other side. Adjust the heat so that each side browns in about 2 minutes; the meat should remain rare. As the pieces finish, put them on a platter and keep them warm in the oven. When they are all done, garnish with parsley, if you like, and serve with lemon wedges, two medallions per serving.

pilaf with pine nuts and currants

This familiar pilaf marries the sweetness of currants with the crunch of pine nuts to gain distinction.

MAKES 8 SERVINGS

TIME: 45 TO 60 MINUTES, LARGELY

UNATTENDED

3 cups chicken, beef, or vegetable stock

3 tablespoons unsalted butter or extra virgin olive oil

1 large onion, chopped

Salt

2 cups white rice, preferably basmati (see Keys to Success)

$1/2$ cup currants or raisins

$1/4$ cup pine nuts

1 teaspoon ground cinnamon

Freshly ground black pepper

$1/2$ cup chopped fresh parsley

1. Gently warm the stock in a small saucepan while you proceed with the recipe. Put the butter in a large, deep skillet that can later be covered and turn the heat to medium. Add the onion and a large pinch of salt and cook, stirring occasionally, until the onion turns translucent, 5 to 10 minutes. Add the rice, currants, pine nuts, and cinnamon and cook, stirring occasionally, until the rice is glossy and begins to brown, 3 to 5 minutes. Season with salt and pepper.

2. Add the warm stock and stir. Raise the heat and bring the mixture to a boil; cook for a minute or two, then reduce the heat to low and cover. Cook about 15 minutes, or until most of the liquid is absorbed. Turn the heat to the absolute minimum (if you have an electric stove, turn the heat off and let the pan sit on the burner) and let the pilaf rest another 15 to 30 minutes. Stir in the parsley and serve.

tender spinach
and crisp shallots

There are a number of ways to make simple dishes of greens more appealing. Among my favorites is to prepare a topping of crisp-fried shallots. By themselves, these are irresistible; when combined with tender greens they create an alluring contrast in flavor and texture. Furthermore, the oil in which the shallots have been fried is a great addition to the greens and, in the days following, to many other dishes.

MAKES 8 SERVINGS

TIME: 30 MINUTES

1 cup or more neutral oil, such as grapeseed, canola, or corn

10 large shallots (8 or more ounces), thinly sliced

Salt and freshly ground black pepper

2 pounds spinach, washed and trimmed

1. Place the oil in a small-to-medium saucepan or narrow, deep skillet; it should be at least an inch deep. Turn the heat to high and wait a few minutes; the oil should reach 350°F. (If you do not have a frying thermometer, just put a couple of slices of shallots in there; when the oil around them bubbles vigorously, it's ready.)

2. Add the shallots and cook, adjusting the heat so that the bubbling is vigorous but not explosive. Cook, stirring, until the shallots begin to darken, 8 to 12 minutes. As soon as they turn golden brown, remove them immediately with a slotted spoon—be careful, because overcooking at this point will burn the shallots. Drain the shallots on paper towels and sprinkle with salt and pepper; they'll keep for a couple of hours this way. Strain the oil; reserve all but 1 tablespoon for another use.

3. Meanwhile, bring a large pot of water to a boil and salt it. When it is ready, add the spinach and cook

(continued)

until it wilts, about 1 minute. Remove the spinach with a strainer or slotted spoon and plunge it into a large bowl filled with ice water to stop the cooking. When it's cool, drain and chop. (You can store the spinach, covered and refrigerated, for up to a couple of days, if you like.)

4. Take 1 tablespoon of the shallot oil and place it in a skillet; turn the heat to medium-high. Turn the spinach into this skillet and cook, stirring frequently and breaking up any clumps, until the spinach is hot, about 5 minutes. Season with salt and pepper and serve, topped with the crisp shallots.

a fast asian dinner

BROILED CORNISH HENS WITH SPICY SALT

STIR-FRIED LEEKS WITH GINGER

EASY RICE (PAGE 180)

HERBED GREEN SALAD WITH SOY VINAIGRETTE (PAGE 38)

COCONUT RICE PUDDING

You're not going to find a menu like this in a typical Asian restaurant: The food is too simple and straightforward. But not only is it fresh and fast, it's unusual and impressive.

KEYS TO SUCCESS

- The Cornish hen recipe is akin to one you often see in eastern Asia, made with squab. If you have access to squab—defined as pigeons who have not yet flown—by all means use them. Not much else will change, except the cooking time: Squab are smaller, and best served medium-rare.

- For the rice pudding, use "sweet" or "sticky" rice, both available at Japanese and most other Asian food markets. If you don't have any, use any short-grain rice.

- Ginger Pots de Crème (page 256) would be another fine meal-ender here.

WINE

Unlike most Asian meals, this one goes pretty well with
European-style wines: Choose a light, dry white like Pinot Blanc,
or a dry rosé from Provence or elsewhere.

THE TIMETABLE

- Make the rice pudding well in advance.

- Prepare the ingredients and the dressing for the salad, and do the chopping for the leeks. Start the rice.

- Make the leeks and serve them with the rice. Cook the hens while you're eating the leeks, and serve them with the salad.

broiled cornish hens with spicy salt

Cornish hens are better-looking, faster to cook, and easier to handle than chickens. With a minimalist spice mix and a broiling technique that involves no turning, they're perfect for a speedy menu. You can find Sichuan peppercorns in many supermarkets and any Asian food market.

MAKES 8 SERVINGS

TIME: 30 TO 40 MINUTES

2 tablespoons Sichuan peppercorns

4 Cornish hens, split in half

Salt

Juice of 2 limes

1. Adjust the broiler rack so that it is about 6 inches from the heating element. Preheat the oven to the maximum, at least 500°F, and put a roasting or broiling pan in it, large enough to hold the birds.

2. Toast the peppercorns in a dry pan over medium heat, shaking occasionally, until fragrant, about 5 minutes. Grind to a powder in a spice mill, coffee grinder, or mortar and pestle. Sprinkle about 1 teaspoon of the powder over the skin side of the hens; sprinkle with a bit of salt as well. Combine the remaining powder with an equal amount of salt and set aside.

3. Turn off the oven and turn on the broiler; carefully remove the pan and put the hens in it, skin side up. Broil without turning, moving the pieces as necessary to brown evenly, for about 20 minutes, or until nicely browned and cooked through.

4. Remove the birds to a plate and drizzle with a little of their pan juices and the lime juice. Serve, passing the spicy salt at the table.

stir-fried leeks with ginger

A big deal is often made of washing leeks but since you're going to be chopping these, it's easy. Start by cutting off the last couple of inches of dark green leaves. Then stand each leek up on its tail and use a sharp knife to "shave" the remaining bits of tough, dark green leaves off the stalk. When only white and pale green leaves remain, cut off the root, slice the leeks in half (or, if they're large, into quarters), and chop them roughly. Then wash in a salad spinner (or a colander inserted into a large bowl) until no traces of sand remain.

MAKES 8 SERVINGS

TIME: 20 MINUTES

$^1/_4$ cup peanut or olive oil

4 large leeks, about 3 pounds, chopped (see headnote)

$^1/_4$ cup minced ginger

Salt and freshly ground black pepper

1 tablespoon soy sauce

1. Put half the oil in a large skillet, preferably nonstick, and turn the heat to high. When a bit of smoke appears, add the leeks, all at once. Let sit for a couple of minutes, then cook, stirring only occasionally, for about 10 minutes.

2. When the leeks dry out and begin to brown, sprinkle with the ginger. Cook, stirring every minute or so, then add some salt (just a little) and pepper, along with the soy sauce. Taste and adjust the seasoning and serve.

coconut rice pudding

Creamier and far more exciting than ordinary rice pudding.

MAKES 8 SERVINGS

TIME: 30 MINUTES

2 cans coconut milk, 3 to 4 cups

1 cup sweet or sticky rice, or any short-grain rice

A tiny pinch of salt

3/4 to 1 cup sugar to taste

1/2 teaspoon ground cinnamon

1. Combine 3 cups coconut milk and the rice in a medium saucepan and bring to a boil over medium heat, stirring occasionally. Add the salt along with 3/4 cup of sugar; reduce the heat to low and cover. Cook for 10 minutes, stirring frequently to make sure the bottom doesn't stick or burn.

2. Uncover and continue to cook, stirring, until the rice is tender and the mixture is creamy, about 15 minutes. If the liquid evaporates before the rice is done, stir in more coconut milk or add water, about 1/2 cup at a time, and cook until done.

3. When the rice is done, the mixture should be sweet and creamy. If it needs more sugar, add it and cook another minute; if it seems dry, stir in a little more coconut milk. Serve warm or cold, sprinkled with the cinnamon.

an informal italian dinner

PASTA WITH FAST SAUSAGE RAGÙ

CHICKEN WITH PANCETTA AND BALSAMIC VINEGAR

PORCINI-SCENTED "WILD" MUSHROOM SAUTÉ

RICOTTA WITH WALNUTS AND HONEY (PAGE 21)

Each of these is a straightforward weeknight dish,
but put them together and you have a restaurant-quality meal
that will impress your guests.

KEYS TO SUCCESS

- If you live near an Italian market, go there for both sausage and pancetta (cured but unsmoked pork belly); you'll probably find porcini sold in bulk there, too. If you do not have pancetta substitute bacon.

- Good balsamic vinegar can also be hard to come by: Shop at a place you trust and, if you can, taste before paying. Though I'm reluctant to recommend specific brands, I have had good luck with the Manicardi line; if you have time for mail order, you might buy from the always-reliable Corti Brothers in Sacramento, California (800–509–3663), trusting them to recommend something good in your price range.

- If you feel like making fresh egg pasta, or can buy it somewhere, this is the ideal pasta recipe in which to use it.

- Herbed Green Salad with Nut Vinaigrette (page 61) will fit the bill if you're looking to add a little green to this menu.

WINE

Chianti, or any other fruity but gutsy red, like zinfandel
or a Côtes du Rhone.

THE TIMETABLE

- It all happens very quickly, and you are going to have to work hard, but only for an hour. Do the little prep work involved first, the chopping and measuring.

- Start the water for the pasta and make the sauce.

- Start the chicken and the mushrooms; the latter can be held warm once they're done.

- While the chicken is browning, cook the pasta. Serve the pasta once you put the chicken in the oven. (If you think it will be more than a few minutes before you get back to the chicken, turn the oven heat to 300°F rather than 400°F. This way you can extend the baking time a bit.)

- Finish the chicken and serve with the mushrooms. Make the dessert after clearing the main course.

pasta with fast sausage ragù

True ragù is a magnificent pasta sauce, a slow-simmered blend of meat, toma-toes, and milk. The real thing takes hours, for the meat must become tender and contribute its silkiness to the sauce, the tomatoes must dissolve, and the milk must pull the whole thing together. But a reasonable approximation of ragù can be produced using ground beef or pork or, even better, prepared Italian sausage.

MAKES 8 SERVINGS

TIME: 30 MINUTES

1 tablespoon extra virgin olive oil

1 large onion, chopped

1 pound Italian sausage, removed from casing if necessary

2 cups milk, more if necessary

$1/2$ cup tomato paste

Salt and freshly ground black pepper

Chicken stock, optional

2 pounds long pasta (fresh, if it's available)

About 2 cups freshly grated Parmesan

1. Set a large pot of water to boil for the pasta. Put the oil in a 10-inch skillet and turn the heat to medium; a minute later add the onion. Cook, stirring occasionally, until it softens, about 5 minutes. Add the sausage in bits and turn the heat to medium-high; cook, stirring infrequently, until the sausage is nicely browned, 5 to 10 minutes.

2. Add the milk and tomato paste, along with some salt and pepper; stir to blend and simmer for about 5 minutes, or until thick but not dry. Keep it warm if necessary and, if it becomes too thick, add a little more milk, water, or chicken stock.

3. Meanwhile, salt the water and cook the pasta. When the pasta is tender but not mushy, drain it. Toss with the sauce and about half the Parmesan. Taste and adjust the seasoning; serve, passing the remaining Parmesan at the table.

chicken with pancetta and balsamic vinegar

A simple dish that is made special by real Italian ingredients.

MAKES 8 SERVINGS

TIME: 45 MINUTES

2 tablespoons extra virgin olive oil

$1/4$ pound pancetta, cut into bits

2 chickens, about 3 pounds each, cut into serving pieces, or 8 legs, cut in two, or 16 thighs

Salt and freshly ground black pepper

16 garlic cloves, peeled and left whole

$1^1/2$ cups white wine or water

$1/4$ cup balsamic vinegar

Minced fresh parsley, optional

1. Turn the oven to 400°F. Put the oil in a large skillet, preferably nonstick, and turn the heat to medium-high. A minute later, add about half the pancetta and cook, stirring occasionally, until it begins to give up some of its fat, just a minute or so. Add as much chicken as will fit comfortably (probably about half), skin side down. Season with salt and pepper and scatter half the garlic in the pan. Quickly brown the chicken on both sides—no more than 10 minutes total—then transfer it, skin side up, to a roasting pan. Repeat the process, adding more oil to the skillet if necessary, and transferring the second batch to the same roasting pan. Put the pan in the oven.

2. When the chicken is all in the oven, make the sauce: Pour off or otherwise remove all but 2 tablespoons of fat from the pan. Add the wine and raise the heat to high. Cook, stirring occasionally and scraping the bottom of the pan if necessary to loosen any browned bits that are stuck there. When the sauce is very thick and glossy, barely covering the bottom of the pan, turn off the heat and stir in the vinegar. When the chicken is cooked through (about 20 minutes; cut into a piece or two if necessary), spoon the sauce (including all the pancetta and garlic) over the chicken, garnish with the parsley, if you like, and serve.

porcini-scented "wild" mushroom sauté

How to get great flavor out of ordinary white mushrooms? Add a handful of dried porcini. You will not believe the difference.

MAKES 8 SERVINGS

TIME: 30 MINUTES

1 cup dried porcini mushrooms

$^1/_2$ cup extra virgin olive oil

2 pounds button mushrooms, cleaned and sliced

Salt and freshly ground black pepper

2 teaspoons minced garlic

$^1/_4$ cup minced fresh parsley leaves

1. Pour boiling water over the porcini mushrooms to reconstitute them; let them sit for about 10 minutes, or until tender, then drain and trim off any hard spots.

2. Put the olive oil in a large skillet and turn the heat to high; a minute later, add the porcini and button mushrooms, along with a big pinch of salt and some pepper, and cook, stirring occasionally, until the mushrooms give off most of their liquid and begin to brown. Turn the heat to medium-low and add the garlic. Continue to cook for a few more minutes, until the mixture is tender and glossy. Taste and adjust the seasoning, stir in the parsley, and serve hot or warm. (You can hold these in a low oven or over *very* low heat for 30 to 60 minutes; stir occasionally.)

a feast from japan

CHAWAN-MUSHI (SAVORY CUSTARD)

SEAWEED SALAD WITH CUCUMBER

JAPANESE-STYLE BEEF STEW WITH WINTER SQUASH

EASY RICE (PAGE 180)

FRUIT

Japanese cuisine is not among the world's most extensive, but it does range beyond the all-too-familiar sushi and teriyaki. This is a meal that includes a couple of unusual dishes—including a traditional savory custard—as well as a homemade version of the ever-popular seaweed salad.

KEYS TO SUCCESS

- Although Chawan-mushi can be made quite legitimately with chicken broth, it's more traditionally made with dashi, the ubiquitous Japanese stock. Here's how to prepare dashi: Slowly heat a 6-inch length of kelp in 2 cups of water until the water is about to boil. Turn off the heat and let sit for 5 minutes. Remove the kelp and gently reheat the water; do not boil. Turn off the heat, add $^1/_2$ cup bonito flakes, let sit for 2 or 3 minutes, and strain.

- The only challenge in making seaweed salad lies in the shopping. Few supermarkets carry any seaweed at all, so you need to hit an Asian or health food market for any kind of selection. In most Japanese markets, and in some health food stores, you can find what amounts to a prepackaged assortment of seaweed salad greens; these are a little more expensive than buying individual seaweeds but will give you a good variety without a big investment.

- While you're at the Japanese market, buy some sesame oil and mirin (sweet rice wine); they'll be less expensive than elsewhere.

- If you want to retain the Japanese theme, but don't want to bother with Chawan-mushi, try Miso-Broiled Scallops (page 198).

WINE

Dry sake would be great, as would a not-perfectly-dry Riesling.

THE TIMETABLE

- This one is a piece of cake. Start by soaking the seaweed, then begin the stew.

- Make the Chawan-mushi (it's fine warm or even at room temperature).

- Prepare a plate of fresh fruit, start the rice, and prepare the seaweed salad.

- Serve the Chawan-mushi first, then the salad, followed by the stew and rice.

chawan-mushi

Chawan-mushi is an egg custard flavored with stock and soy and laced with a number of tasty tidbits. In Tokyo, I had a bowl that contained tiny amounts of myoga (a potent member of the onion family), shrimp, chicken, and gingko nut. None of these is essential, and you can substitute for any or all of them, as I do in the recipe below.

MAKES 8 SERVINGS

TIME: 30 MINUTES

24 leaves watercress

8 sea scallops, each cut into 4 pieces

4 shallots, chopped

Salt and freshly ground black pepper

8 eggs

3 cups chicken or beef stock or dashi (see Keys to Success)

2 tablespoons soy sauce

1. Put one-eighth each of the watercress, scallops, and shallots in each of eight 6-ounce ramekins and sprinkle with salt and pepper. Beat the eggs lightly and combine with the stock and soy.

2. Put the ramekins in a deep baking pan or skillet and fill them with the egg mixture. Add boiling water about halfway up the height of the ramekins and turn the heat to high. When the water returns to the boil, turn the heat to low, and cover tightly.

3. Simmer for 15 minutes, then check. The custards are done when they have set and are no longer watery, but are still quite jiggly. Remove them from the water immediately, and serve hot, warm, or at room temperature.

seaweed salad with cucumber

This is simply a kind of sea-based mesclun with a distinctively sesame-flavored dressing. You can use leftover chicken (or shrimp) or cook it expressly for this purpose; start with about a pound of boneless chicken or shrimp and steam, grill, broil, roast, or pan-grill until done, less than 10 minutes. (You can also omit the chicken or shrimp entirely; the salad is delicious without it.)

To toast sesame seeds, heat them in a dry skillet over medium heat, shaking occasionally, until they brown lightly and begin to pop.

MAKES 8 SERVINGS

TIME: 20 MINUTES

2 ounces wakame or assorted seaweeds

1 pound cucumber, preferably Kirby, English, or Japanese

1 pound shredded cooked chicken or roughly chopped cooked shrimp, optional

1/2 cup minced shallots, scallions, or red onion

1/4 cup soy sauce

2 tablespoons rice wine or other light vinegar

2 tablespoons mirin

2 tablespoons sesame oil

1/2 teaspoon cayenne, or to taste

Salt, if necessary

2 tablespoons toasted sesame seeds, optional

1. Rinse the seaweed once and soak it in at least ten times its volume of water.

2. Wash and dice the cucumber; do not peel unless necessary. When the seaweed is tender, 5 minutes later, drain and gently squeeze the mixture to remove the excess water. Pick through the seaweed to sort out any hard bits (there may be none), and chop or cut up (you can use scissors, which you may find easier) if the pieces are large. Combine the cucumber and seaweed mixture in a bowl; add chicken or shrimp (if desired) to the bowl.

3. Toss with the remaining ingredients except the sesame seeds; taste and add salt or other seasonings as necessary, and serve, garnished with the sesame seeds, if you're using.

japanese-style beef stew with winter squash

You can make this much more quickly by substituting beef tenderloin for the chuck; cooking time will be less than a half hour.

MAKES 8 SERVINGS

TIME: AT LEAST 1 HOUR, LARGELY UNATTENDED

3 to 4 pounds boneless chuck, cut into 1- to 1$^{1}/_{2}$-inch chunks

4 cups chicken stock or dashi (see Keys to Success)

$^{1}/_{2}$ cup soy sauce

$^{1}/_{2}$ cup mirin, honey, or sugar

20 nickel-sized slices of ginger

Freshly ground black pepper

2 lemons

3 pounds peeled butternut, pumpkin, or other winter squash or sweet potatoes, cut into 1-inch chunks

Salt, if necessary

1. Sear the meat in a large skillet, preferably nonstick, over medium-high heat, until nicely browned; do it in two or three batches to avoid crowding. It will take only 5 minutes per batch, since it's sufficient to brown the meat well on one side. As you finish, transfer the chunks to a medium casserole.

2. When the meat is all browned, add the stock to the skillet and cook over high heat, stirring and scraping occasionally, until all the solids are integrated into the liquid. Pour into the casserole with the soy sauce, mirin, ginger, and a couple of grindings of pepper. Peel the lemon and add the peel to the mixture; juice the lemon and reserve the juice.

3. Cover and cook on top of the stove (or in a preheated 350°F oven), maintaining a steady simmer. Stir after 30 minutes and begin to check the meat at 15-minute intervals. (If you're using tenderloin, add the squash immediately and stop cooking when the squash is done.)

4. When the meat is tender, or nearly so, stir in the squash and continue to cook as before, checking every 15 minutes, until the squash is tender but not mushy. Add salt, if necessary, then stir in the reserved lemon juice and serve.

a leisurely midwinter dinner

WHITE BEAN DIP (PAGE 196)

SLOW-COOKED LEG OF LAMB WITH FRESH MINT SAUCE

GREEN BEANS AND TOMATOES

FAST POTATO GRATIN

FREE-FORM APPLE OR PEAR TART (PAGE 237)

This is real cold-weather food, slow-cooked and rich. There are some shortcuts—most notably the fast, delicious gratin and the tart—and none of the dishes is difficult. The centerpiece is a slow-cooked leg of lamb, an item that is cooked undisturbed for hours, and which can be finished in as "little" as 6 hours or as many as 8 or 10. (You can literally make it in your sleep.) Considering the amount of work, the payoff is amazing.

KEYS TO SUCCESS

- The lamb can be cooked most of the way and then set aside for a few hours (tented with aluminum foil), to be finished just before eating, or it can be held in a very low oven for an hour or even two (covered) after it is done.

- Do not use baking potatoes for the gratin, but either waxy new potatoes or "all-purpose" potatoes like Yukon Gold. Idaho baking potatoes will fall apart.

WINE

Red, and the best you can find; this is a meal worthy of one of those special wines you have been hoarding. If you're buying, and you want to save money, go with a decent Rioja. If you are splurging, look for a classified Bordeaux that is at its peak.

THE TIMETABLE

- You can do anything you want for the first few hours after starting the lamb. Cook the beans, prepare the crust for the tart, trim the green beans, make the mint sauce, or watch a movie.

- A little over an hour before you're ready to eat, start the green beans and make the bean dip. Then start the gratin.

- Just before serving the dip, prepare the tart; bake it while you're eating.

slow-cooked leg of lamb with fresh mint sauce

Although the meat is well done it's beyond tender (you can just about serve it with a spoon) and quite moist, especially when topped with some of the pan juices.

MAKES 8 SERVINGS

TIME: ABOUT 6 HOURS, LARGELY

UNATTENDED

1 tablespoon coarse salt

4 large garlic cloves

1 whole leg of lamb, about
6 pounds, trimmed of excess fat

Freshly ground black pepper

$1/2$ cup sherry vinegar

$1/3$ cup sugar

2 cups fresh mint leaves

1. Preheat the oven to 250°F. Mince together the salt and garlic (if you have a small food processor, use it); with a small, sharp knife, poke holes all over the lamb and insert some of this mixture into each hole. Smear any of the remaining mixture on the lamb's skin, then sprinkle with additional salt, if necessary, and pepper. Place the lamb in a roasting pan, cover it lightly with aluminum foil, and put it in the oven. Cook for 4 hours, then remove the foil. Cook for about 2 more hours, until a sharp, thin-bladed knife can be easily inserted into the meat. (See Keys to Success for more flexibility in cooking times.) If the lamb's skin is not nicely browned, raise the heat to 400°F for 10 minutes or so.

2. To make the mint sauce, combine the vinegar and sugar in a small saucepan with $1/3$ cup water and a pinch of salt. Bring to a boil and cook for about 30 seconds longer. Cool for a few minutes, then combine in the container of a blender with the mint; blend until smooth. Keep at room temperature until ready to serve (or refrigerate overnight and return to room temperature before serving).

3. Carve the lamb and spoon some of the pan juices over the slices. Serve hot, passing the sauce at the table.

green beans and tomatoes

With the slow-cooked lamb I like slow-cooked green beans, an eastern Mediterranean-style dish using a technique that makes the beans soft and sweet.

MAKES 8 SERVINGS

TIME: AT LEAST 1 HOUR, LARGELY
UNATTENDED

2 tablespoons extra virgin olive oil

2 pounds green beans, washed
and trimmed

2 pints cherry or grape tomatoes,
washed

Salt and freshly ground black
pepper

1. Put 1 tablespoon of olive oil in a large skillet and turn the heat to high. Add the beans and cook, undisturbed, until they begin to brown a little on the bottom. Add the tomatoes, turn the heat to low, and cover. Cook about an hour, stirring occasionally, until the beans are very tender. (You can cook even more slowly if you like, or cook until done, turn off the heat, and reheat gently just before serving.)

2. Season with salt and pepper and stir in the remaining olive oil. Serve hot or at room temperature.

fast potato gratin

This is a fast method for producing a delicious potato gratin. I discovered it accidentally and it's since become a personal favorite.

MAKES 8 SERVINGS

TIME: 40 MINUTES

4 pounds all-purpose potatoes

Salt and freshly ground black pepper

2 teaspoons minced garlic, or a grating of nutmeg, optional

4 tablespoons ($1/2$ stick) unsalted butter

5 to 6 cups half-and-half or milk, or more

1. Peel the potatoes and rinse them; slice them thinly with a knife or mandoline. Layer them in a large nonstick, ovenproof skillet or roasting pan, sprinkling between the layers with salt and pepper and, if you like, the garlic. Dot with the butter, then add enough half-and-half to come about three-quarters of the way up to the top. Preheat the oven to 400°F.

2. Turn the heat under the potatoes to high and bring to a boil. Lower the heat to medium-high and cook for about 10 minutes, or until the level of both liquid and potatoes has subsided somewhat. Put in the oven and cook, undisturbed, until the top is nicely browned, about 10 minutes. Turn the oven heat down to 300° and continue cooking until the potatoes are tender (a thin-bladed knife will pierce them with little or no resistance), about 10 minutes more. Serve immediately or keep warm in the oven or over a very low flame for up to 30 minutes.

a light and elegant midwinter meal

GARLIC-MUSHROOM FLAN

ROASTED BAY SCALLOPS WITH BROWN BUTTER AND SHALLOTS

ENDIVES BRAISED IN BROTH WITH PARMESAN

FREE-FORM APPLE OR PEAR TART

Here's a change: a light winter meal that is not at all insubstantial. The savory custard is pretty rich, as is the dessert. In between are relatively lean preparations of scallops and endives. All in all, it's a graceful menu.

KEYS TO SUCCESS

- Real Parmesan is essential to the endive dish; you can, however, get away with using canned stock.

- If this menu seems too light for you, add Poached Beef Tenderloin with Garnishes (page 248).

- The free-form tart, rich with butter, is a substantial dessert, but it becomes even more so when served with crème fraîche, whipped cream, or ice cream.

WINE

The best white you can lay your hands on, which almost always means a Burgundy, in this case something from the area of Montrachet or Meursault, if you can afford it.

THE TIMETABLE

- I like the tart hot, or at least warm, which means I delay assembling and baking it until after eating the rest of the meal. But make the dough early on.

- Make the flans (which can be served hot or at room temperature) while you ready the scallops and endives.

- After eating the flans, brown the endives and set aside; keep warm while you roast the scallops.

garlic-mushroom flan

We usually think of custards as desserts, but they may be savory as well, and in that form make luxurious starters or light, flavorful main courses. Custards like garlic flan are often served in top restaurants, but the simplicity and ease of this preparation makes them good options for home cooks. Here's one with a surprise in it: cooked shiitakes. It will be a hit.

MAKES 8 SERVINGS

TIME: 40 MINUTES

2 tablespoons unsalted butter

1 teaspoon minced garlic

1 cup thinly sliced shiitake mushrooms (caps only; stems should be reserved for stock or discarded)

Salt and freshly ground black pepper

3 cups chicken or beef stock

8 eggs

1. Put the butter in a medium saucepan and turn the heat to medium. Add the garlic and mushrooms and cook, stirring occasionally and sprinkling with salt and pepper, until the garlic is fragrant and the mushrooms begin to soften, just 5 minutes or so. Stir in the stock.

2. Beat the eggs lightly and add a bit of the stock mixture. Beat, then add the remaining stock. Put about an inch of water in a baking pan or skillet just large enough to hold eight 6-ounce ramekins and turn the heat to high. When the water boils, turn the heat to low, pour the egg mixture into the ramekins, and put the ramekins in the water. Cover tightly with foil and/or a lid.

3. Simmer for 15 to 20 minutes, then check; the moment the custards are set—they should still be quite jiggly—remove them from the water. Serve hot or at room temperature.

roasted bay scallops with brown butter and shallots

Real bay scallops—the kind that come mostly from Nantucket—are in season through the winter, and are an amazing treat (they're also expensive). Though you can eat them raw, they're also good cooked, but simply . . . very simply. Substitute sea scallops if you like, but, if they're big, cut them into halves or quarters.

MAKES 8 SERVINGS

TIME: 20 MINUTES

1 stick unsalted butter

3 pounds bay or sea scallops

1/4 cup minced shallots

Salt and freshly ground black pepper

Chopped fresh basil or snipped fresh chives

1. Preheat the oven to the maximum, at least 500°F. Put a roasting pan large enough to hold the scallops in one layer in the oven while it preheats. When the oven is hot, add the butter to the pan. Cook, shaking the pan once or twice, until the butter melts and begins to turn brown.

2. Immediately add the scallops and cook, undisturbed, about 3 minutes. Remove the pan, add the shallots, and stir. Return to the oven for about 2 minutes, or until the scallops are done cooking (they should be tender and not at all rubbery; do not overcook). Season with salt and pepper, stir in the herb, and serve.

endives braised in broth with parmesan

Grown indoors in the dark, endives are among the perfect winter vegetables, usually used in salads but also lovely when cooked. This simple gratin benefits from good, dark stock, but the addition of Parmesan will cover you if you resort to canned stock.

MAKES 8 SERVINGS

TIME: 40 MINUTES

8 whole Belgian endives

2 cups good stock

Salt and freshly ground black pepper

$^1/_2$ cup freshly grated Parmesan

1. Remove and discard just a couple of the outer leaves from each of the endives; rinse the endives and put them in an ovenproof skillet large enough to hold them in one layer. Add the stock and sprinkle with salt and pepper. Cover and cook over medium heat until tender, 20 to 30 minutes. Preheat the broiler.

2. Cover the endives with the Parmesan and run under the broiler, just long enough to slightly brown the cheese. Serve with a slotted spoon.

free-form apple
or pear tart

The most difficult part of many tarts is shaping the shell; by eliminating that task, this becomes a snap. And it tastes no less wonderful for it.

MAKES 8 SERVINGS

TIME: ABOUT 2 HOURS, LARGELY
UNATTENDED

1¼ cups all-purpose flour

Pinch of salt

3 tablespoons sugar

9 tablespoons cold unsalted butter

1 egg yolk

3 or 4 medium apples or pears, peeled, cored, and very thinly sliced

2 tablespoons brown sugar

1. Combine the flour, salt, and sugar in the container of a food processor; pulse once or twice. Cut 8 tablespoons of the butter into chunks and add it and the egg yolk to the flour mixture. Turn on the machine; process until the butter and flour are blended, about 10 seconds. Turn the mixture into a bowl and add cold water, a tablespoon at a time, stirring after each addition. After adding 3 or 4 tablespoons you should be able to gather the mixture into a ball; do so, wrap in plastic, and refrigerate for at least an hour (or freeze for about 15 minutes).

2. Preheat the oven to 400°F. Roll or pat the dough into a rough, 10-inch circle; it can be quite crude in shape. Place it on a cookie or pizza sheet, preferably nonstick. Arrange the fruit slices on top, almost out to the edges; fold the edges themselves up a little to form a border. If you work from the center out you can make an attractive pattern. Sprinkle with the brown sugar. Cut the remaining butter into bits and top the fruit with it.

3. Bake until the crust is nicely browned and the fruit is tender, 20 to 30 minutes. Remove and serve warm or at room temperature.

a dinner
from north africa

SHRIMP IN MOROCCAN-STYLE TOMATO SAUCE

SAUTÉED CHICKPEAS WITH MEAT

EASY RICE (PAGE 180) OR BREAD

MACERATED DRIED FRUIT

Like some Indian cuisine, that of Morocco
is readily identified by its sweet and pungent spice mixtures.
These easy dishes combine to give the meal an exotic air.

KEYS TO SUCCESS

- Almost all spices are best when lightly toasted and ground just before using, and this is an excellent place to practice that axiom. If you have cumin and coriander seeds, cook them in a dry skillet over medium heat, shaking the pan occasionally, until fragrant, less than 5 minutes. Then grind in a clean spice mill or coffee grinder.

- Since you will be using the chickpea liquid, it's preferable to cook the chickpeas from scratch—allow plenty of time, because chickpeas can take a few hours to become tender. (You can reduce the cooking time somewhat by soaking them in water to cover overnight—or for 6 to 8 hours—but it isn't necessary.)

- Lime leaves are sometimes sold fresh in Indian or North African markets. Dried lime leaves are not nearly as good—use lime zest instead.

WINE

Rough, inexpensive red from the south of France,
California, or Italy is best here.

THE TIMETABLE

- Start with the fruit, the day before if you like. Cook the chickpeas a day early if you think of it, too.

- Prepare the sauce for the shrimp.

- Cook the chickpea dish through Step 2. Finish and serve the shrimp, then finish the chickpeas and serve them.

shrimp in moroccan-style tomato sauce

The main ingredients are standard and the technique and appearance are standard. The seasonings, however, are not from Italy but the other side of the Mediterranean. And that's the key: By substituting a couple of different spices, most or all of which you have sitting in your kitchen already, you can transform the common into the exotic.

MAKES 8 SERVINGS

TIME: 40 MINUTES

1/4 cup olive oil

2 tablespoons minced ginger

2 tablespoons ground cumin

1 tablespoon ground coriander

2 minced fresh lime leaves, or
2 teaspoons minced lime zest (see
Keys to Success)

One 35-ounce can chopped
tomatoes, drained, or 5 cups
chopped fresh tomatoes

Salt and freshly ground black
pepper

3 pounds peeled shrimp,
deveined if you like

Minced cilantro

Lime wedges

1. Put the olive oil in a large, deep skillet and turn the heat to medium-high. A minute later, add the ginger and cook, stirring, for about a minute. Add the spices and the lime leaves or zest and cook, stirring, for 30 seconds. Add the tomatoes and some salt and pepper, stir, and bring to a boil. Reduce the heat to medium and cook, stirring occasionally, until the mixture is nearly dry, about 15 minutes.

2. Add the shrimp and stir. Cook, stirring occasionally, until the shrimp are cooked through, about 10 minutes.

3. Taste and adjust the seasoning as necessary, then serve over white rice, garnished with the cilantro and accompanied by the lime wedges.

sautéed chickpeas with meat

This recipe, which is vaguely related to the more common chili, combines chickpeas, meat, and spices, and takes advantage of all of those assets. The cooked chickpeas are sautéed over high heat until browned and slightly crisp, and the pan is ultimately deglazed with the reserved chickpea cooking liquid.

TIME: 30 MINUTES (WITH CANNED OR PRECOOKED CHICKPEAS)

1 pound ground beef or other meat

8 cups cooked chickpeas, drained (reserve 2 cups of their cooking or canning liquid)

1 tablespoon ground cumin

1 ancho or chipotle chile, soaked, stemmed, seeded, and minced, or 2 teaspoons good chili powder, or to taste

1 tablespoon minced garlic

Salt and freshly ground black pepper

2 tablespoons extra virgin olive oil

Minced cilantro or fresh parsley, optional

1. Turn the heat to high under a large, deep skillet and add the meat a little at a time, breaking it into small pieces as you do so. Stir and break up the meat a bit more, then add the chickpeas. Keep the heat high and continue to cook, stirring only occasionally until the chickpeas begin to brown and pop, 5 to 10 minutes. Don't worry if the mixture sticks a bit, but if it begins to scorch lower the heat slightly.

2. Add the cumin, chile, and garlic, and cook, stirring, for about a minute. Add the reserved cooking liquid and stir, scraping the bottom of the pan if necessary to loosen any browned bits that have stuck. Season with salt and pepper, then turn the heat to medium-low; continue to cook until the mixture is no longer soupy but not completely dry, about 10 minutes.

3. Stir in the olive oil, then taste and adjust the seasoning if necessary. Garnish, if you like, and serve immediately, with rice or pita breads.

macerated dried fruit

This recipe, adapted from a classic by Claudia Roden, is a longtime personal favorite. It becomes heavenly if you add a little rose and/or orange-flower water.

MAKES AT LEAST 8 SERVINGS

TIME: 6 TO 48 HOURS, LARGELY UNATTENDED

2 pounds assorted dried fruit: apricots, pears, peaches, prunes, raisins, etc.

$1/2$ cup pine nuts or slivered blanched almonds

1 tablespoon rose water, optional

1 tablespoon orange-flower water, optional

$1/2$ cup sugar, or to taste

Sour cream or crème fraîche

1. Combine everything but the sour cream in a bowl and add water to cover. Stir and let sit, at room temperature, for at least 6 hours. The fruit is ready when it is soft and the liquid is syrupy.

2. To serve, put some fruit in a bowl and garnish with sour cream.

an old-fashioned menu

REAL ONION SOUR CREAM DIP

SHRIMP WITH BETTER COCKTAIL SAUCE

POACHED BEEF TENDERLOIN WITH GARNISHES

STEAMED BROCCOLI WITH BEURRE NOISETTE

MAPLE BREAD PUDDING

The menu here is perfect for a nice, small party where you don't want to fuss or take any risks. If your guests are less adventurous, or you just want a break from contemporary food—and from hard work—this retro menu should do the trick.

KEYS TO SUCCESS

- Poaching beef is foolproof, and produces gorgeous, rosy pink meat throughout. There is one caveat, however: The piece of beef you choose must be of uniform thickness, or it will not cook evenly. (If you know that one of your guests wants well-done meat, this could be a good thing—an uneven piece will give you meat of differing degrees of doneness. But tenderloin is at its best medium-rare.)

- Maple Bread Pudding becomes ordinary bread pudding if you don't have real maple syrup; use sugar instead of imitation maple syrup.

WINE

This could be a two-wine meal: A Champagne or crisp white
to open the show, served with the dip and shrimp cocktail, followed
by a good, sturdy red for the beef.

THE TIMETABLE

- Much of this menu can be made far in advance, up to a day; the bread pudding, the shrimp, the cocktail sauce, and the dip.

- You can start the meat before serving the shrimp or, if you're having a more leisurely dinner, after eating it. The broccoli can be made ahead, but the beurre noisette should be prepared at the last minute.

real onion sour cream dip

As you can imagine, substituting freshly cooked crisp onions makes a far better dip than using dried onion soup mix.

MAKES ABOUT 1 CUP, ENOUGH FOR
ABOUT 8 SERVINGS

TIME: 15 MINUTES

$^{1}/_{3}$ cup neutral oil, such as canola or grapeseed

1 medium onion, minced, about $^{1}/_{2}$ cup

Pinch of salt

$^{1}/_{4}$ teaspoon sugar

1 cup sour cream

1. Place the oil in an 8-inch skillet and turn the heat to medium-high. When it's hot, a minute or two later, add the onion, salt, and sugar. Cook, shaking the pan occasionally, until the onion browns, about 10 minutes.

2. Pour the onion and oil into a fine strainer; reserve the oil for another use (refrigerate it in the meantime). Stir the onion into the sour cream; cover and refrigerate for 24 hours or so if time allows. Serve with potato chips or cut-up vegetables.

shrimp with better cocktail sauce

This is a rich cocktail sauce, laced with butter but made spiky with vinegar and horseradish—make it as hot as you like, and serve it warm or cold.

MAKES 8 SERVINGS

TIME: 30 MINUTES

3 pounds large shrimp, peeled

1 cup ketchup

1 tablespoon vinegar

3 tablespoons unsalted butter

2 tablespoons prepared horseradish, or to taste

1. Put the shrimp in a saucepan with water to cover. Turn the heat to high and bring to a boil. Cover the pan, remove from the heat, and let sit for 10 minutes. Drain and chill (you can run under cold water if you're in a hurry).

2. Combine the ketchup, vinegar, and butter in a small saucepan and cook over medium-low heat, stirring occasionally, until the butter melts. (At this point, you can keep the sauce warm for an hour—but make the heat as low as possible.) Add the horseradish.

3. Serve the cold shrimp with the warm or cold sauce.

poached beef tenderloin with garnishes

Serve the meat with a variety of garnishes, from which you and your guests can choose: minced shallots, good mustard, chopped cornichons, coarse salt, soy sauce, even ketchup. These can be combined any way you like.

MAKES 8 SERVINGS

TIME: 30 MINUTES

One 3- to 4-pound piece beef tenderloin, from the thick end, preferably at room temperature

6 cups stock or water, heated

Salt, if necessary

Garnishes, such as minced shallots, good mustard, chopped cornichons, coarse salt, soy sauce, and ketchup

1. Put the meat in a deep pan just large enough to fit it—a Dutch oven is usually ideal, but you can curve the meat into a wide saucepan, too—and cover it with the hot stock or water. Add a large pinch of salt if you're using water or if the stock is unsalted. Adjust the heat so that the mixture bubbles gently—on my stove that's medium.

2. Cook for about 10 minutes, then check the temperature. The meat is done when its internal temperature reaches 125°F (use an instant-read thermometer); 120°F if you prefer very rare. Remove the meat and let it sit for about 5 minutes, then cut into $1/2$- to 1-inch-thick slices. Serve immediately, with the garnishes.

steamed broccoli
with beurre noisette

If you've never had beurre noisette—essentially browned butter—its complex nutty (noisette means nutlike) flavor and beguiling aroma will amaze you.

MAKES 8 SERVINGS

TIME: 30 MINUTES

2 to 3 pounds broccoli

6 tablespoons unsalted butter

Salt and freshly ground black pepper

Olive oil or butter for reheating the broccoli, optional

1 tablespoon fresh lemon juice

1. Trim the broccoli as necessary (the thick stems should be peeled with a vegetable peeler or paring knife to make them less tough). Cut the stems and florets into equal-size pieces.

2. Put the butter in a small saucepan and turn the heat to medium. Cook, swirling the pan occasionally, until the butter stops foaming and begins to brown. Remove from the heat immediately and season lightly with salt and pepper; keep warm if necessary.

3. Steam the broccoli over boiling water or boil in salted water to cover until tender and bright green, usually less than 10 minutes. Drain if necessary and sprinkle with salt. (Or run under cold water and refrigerate. To reheat, put a little olive oil or butter in a pan over medium heat and turn the broccoli in it until hot.) Swirl the lemon juice into the beurre noisette and drizzle it over the broccoli; serve immediately.

maple bread pudding

Use good white bread for this, and don't bother to remove the crusts; the different textures make it more interesting.

MAKES 8 SERVINGS

TIME: ABOUT 1 HOUR, LARGELY
UNATTENDED

8 tablespoons (1 stick) unsalted butter

1 pound white bread, cut or torn into chunks no smaller than 1 inch in diameter

2 cups milk

2 cups cream, or a total of 4 cups half-and-half

8 eggs

1¼ cups maple syrup or sugar

1 teaspoon ground cinnamon

Small grating of nutmeg

Pinch of salt

1. Use some of the butter to grease a 10- or 12-inch soufflé or baking dish and put the bread in it. Cut the remaining butter into bits and combine it with all the other ingredients; pour over the bread. Submerge the bread with a plate weighted with a couple of cans and turn the oven to 350°F.

2. When the oven is hot, remove the plate (scrape off any butter back onto the bread) and bake until the pudding is just set but not dry, 45 to 60 minutes. The top will be crusty and brown. Serve hot, warm, or at room temperature, with or without whipped cream.

a fast
pan-asian sit-down

STEAMED SHRIMP WITH LEMONGRASS-COCONUT SAUCE

BEEF WITH CARAMELIZED SUGAR

EASY RICE (PAGE 180)

SEAWEED SALAD WITH CUCUMBER (PAGE 223)

GINGER POTS DE CRÈME

Like A Fast Asian Dinner on page 208, this is a meal of simple Asian dishes with clean, bright distinctive flavors; it is, however, a tad more formal. Which does not mean it's difficult, just that it's slightly more impressive. The shrimp is a cold dish, a great starter, but the beef is super-hearty. Ginger Pots de Crème are surprising and fabulous.

KEYS TO SUCCESS

■ Fresh lemongrass is sold, increasingly, in supermarkets, and almost always in good Asian food markets. Dried lemongrass, I'm sorry to say, is nearly worthless.

■ Make the Seaweed Salad with Cucumber (page 223) without added protein for this menu.

■ Caramel can be tricky to make, but if you add a little water to the sugar before beginning, you'll be successful. If the caramel sticks to the pan, put some water in it and heat on the stove for fast cleanup.

WINE

Serve a fruity Riesling, very cold, or a not-too-dry rosé,
also chilled. Or good beer.

THE TIMETABLE

■ Make the pots de crème as far in advance as you like, up to a day. Except for making the caramel, the beef can be prepared early on also. Steam the shrimp and make their sauce; chill.

■ Start the beef. Make the seaweed salad and start the rice.

■ Keep the beef and rice warm while you serve the shrimp; then serve the beef, rice, and salad.

steamed shrimp with lemongrass-coconut sauce

Dealing with the lemongrass is the sole challenge inherent in this dish, and that is the case only if you've never done it before. Maximum flavor is released from whole lemongrass stalks when they are beat up a bit; bruising the length of each stalk with the blunt edge of a knife takes care of this in seconds. But to use a stalk of lemongrass you must first remove the tough, outer layers—this is not unlike peeling a woody scallion—and then carefully and finely mince the inner core.

MAKES 8 SERVINGS

TIME: 30 MINUTES, PLUS TIME TO CHILL

4 lemongrass stalks

2 tablespoons nam pla (Thai fish sauce)

3 limes

2 pounds shrimp, peeled

1 dried chile

1 cup coconut milk

1 tablespoon sugar

1 large pinch of saffron, or
1 teaspoon turmeric or curry powder

Salt, if necessary

1. Trim the ends from the lemongrass, then bruise three of the stalks all over with the back of a knife. Cut them in half and put them in the bottom of a saucepan with the nam pla. Squeeze the juice of two of the limes into the pot, then add the limes themselves. Top with the shrimp, cover tightly, and turn the heat to medium-high. Cook for 5 to 10 minutes, or until the shrimp are pink and firm. Remove the shrimp and chill.

2. Remove the hard outer layers from the remaining lemongrass stalk and mince the tender core; you won't get much more than a teaspoon or two. Combine this with the chile, coconut milk, sugar, and saffron in a small saucepan over low heat. Cook, stirring occasionally, until the mixture is a uniform yellow, just a few minutes. Remove the chile and chill the sauce. Cut the remaining lime into wedges.

3. Taste the chilled sauce and add a little salt if necessary. Serve the cold shrimp topped with the cold sauce and accompanied by lime wedges.

beef with caramelized sugar

Caramel is the key to what makes this dish distinctive; though it is made from sugar, it gains a certain bitterness if you cook it long enough. Chances are no one will be able to figure out how you made this.

MAKES 8 SERVINGS

TIME: 2 HOURS OR LESS

One 4-pound piece boneless chuck roast

2 large onions, sliced

Salt and freshly ground black pepper

2 cups stock or water

2 cups sugar

2 lemons

2 tablespoons soy sauce

1. Heat a large, deep skillet over medium-high heat for a couple of minutes, then add the beef. Sear on one side until nicely browned, about 5 minutes, then sear on the other side. Remove to a plate, turn the heat to medium, and add the onions. Season them with salt and pepper and cook, stirring occasionally, until they are tender, 5 to 10 minutes.

2. Return the meat to the pan and season it with more salt and pepper; add the stock, bring to a boil, turn the heat to low, and cover the pan. It should bubble steadily but not vigorously. Cook until the meat is tender, at least an hour.

3. When the meat is done, put the sugar in a small, heavy saucepan over medium-high heat; add a couple of tablespoons of water. Cook, shaking the pan occasionally, until the sugar melts and turns dark golden brown. Carefully add about half the caramel to the simmering beef and stir. Slice one of the lemons and add it, along with the soy sauce. If the mixture is appealingly salty and bitter, it is done; if it is tame, add more salt, pepper, and/or some of the caramel (discard remaining caramel). Juice the remaining lemon and add the juice, to taste, to the sauce. Carve the meat and serve it with the sauce.

ginger pots de crème

Pots de crème are always great, but flavored with ginger they become exotic. Yet there's nothing to it.

MAKES 8 SERVINGS

TIME: ABOUT 1 HOUR

4 cups heavy cream, light cream, or half-and-half

20 ginger slices

10 egg yolks

1 cup sugar

2 tablespoons minced candied ginger, optional

1. Preheat the oven to 300°F. Combine the cream and fresh ginger in a small saucepan and heat over medium-low heat until steam rises. Cover the pan, turn off the heat, and let steep for 10 to 15 minutes.

2. Beat the yolks and sugar together until light. Remove the ginger slices and pour about a quarter of the cream into this mixture, then pour the sugar-egg mixture into the cream and stir. If you're using the candied ginger, add it now. Pour into eight 6-ounce ramekins and place the ramekins in a baking dish; fill the dish with water halfway up the sides of the ramekins and cover with foil.

3. Bake for 30 to 45 minutes, or until the center is barely set. (Heavy cream sets up fastest; half-and-half more slowly.) Cool or chill, then serve.

Index